P9-CQM-339

GO GAMING!

THE ULTIMATE GUIDE TO THE WORLD'S GREATEST MOBILE GAMES

GO GAMING!

EDITOR IN CHIEF
Jon White

EDITOR
Dan Peel

WRITERS
Luke Albigés, Wesley Copeland,
David Crookes, Fraser Gilbert,
Craig Grannell, Andrew Hayward,
Ryan King, Paul Walker-Emig,
Alan Wen, Josh West

LEAD DESIGNER
Adam Markiewicz

DESIGNERS
Steve Dacombe, Andy Downes,
Rebekka Hearl, Harriet Knight,
Newton Ribeiro, Katy Stokes,
Jordan Travers, Kimberly Winters

PRODUCTION
Alex Burrows, Russell Lewin,
Nikole Robinson

Copyright © 2019 by Scholastic Inc.
All rights reserved. Published by
Scholastic Inc., Publishers since 1920.
Scholastic and associated logos are
trademarks and/or registered trademarks
of Scholastic Inc.
No part of this publication may be
reproduced, stored in a retrieval
system, or transmitted in any form or
by any means, electronic, mechanical,
photocopying, recording, or otherwise,
without written permission of the
publisher. For information regarding
permission, write to Scholastic Inc.,
Attention: Permissions Department,
557 Broadway, New York, NY 10012.

The publisher does not have any
control over and does not assume any
responsibility for author or third party
websites or their content, including the
websites of any brands, gamers and social
media personalities included in this book.

ISBN 978-1-338-31644-5
10 9 8 7 6 5 4 3 2 1   15 16 17 18 19
Printed in the U.S.A.   40
First printing, January 2019

Scholastic is constantly working to
lessen the environmental impact of our
manufacturing processes. To view our
industry-leading paper procurement
policy, visit www.scholastic.com/
paperpolicy.

COVER IMAGES

Holedown © webbfarbror AB 2018
The Big Journey © Armor Games Inc. All
Rights Reserved.
Lumino City © State of Play
Alphabear 2 © Spry Fox 2018
Flat Pack is copyright of Nitrome Limited
Hello Neighbor © tinyBuild, LLC. All
Rights Reserved. © 2018 DYNAMIC
PIXELS™
Silly Walks © Part Time Monkey 2018
Pocket City © Codebrew Games 2018
Dandara © 2018 Raw Fury AB
Monument Valley 2 © ustwo Games 2017
Morphite © 2011 Blowfish Studios | Level
77 Pty Ltd
Vikings: An Archer's Journey © Pinpin
Team 2018
Old Man's Journey - image courtesy of
Broken Rules
Roblox © 2018 Roblox Corp. ROBLOX is a
registered mark
Alto's Odyssey © Snowman 2018
Arkanoid vs Space Invaders © TAITO
Corporation 1978, 2017 ALL RIGHTS
RESERVED
Poly Bridge © 2016 Dry Cactus. All rights
reserved.
Ocmo © 2017 teamocmo.com
Splitter Critters © RAC7 2018
Battle of Polytopia © Midjiwan AB
Minecraft © 2018 Microsoft, Inc. All rights
reserved.

Linelight © My Dog Zorro., 2015 – 2018
Asphalt 9: Legends © 2018 Gameloft. All
Rights Reserved. Gameloft, the Gameloft
logo and Asphalt are trademarks of
Gameloft in the U.S. and/or other
countries. All manufacturers, cars,
names, brands and associated imagery
featured in the Asphalt 9: Legends
mobile game are trademarks and/or
copyrighted materials of their respective
owners.
Frost © kunabi brother 2018
Lara Croft GO ©2015 SQUARE ENIX LTD.
LARA CROFT and LARA CROFT GO are
trademarks of Square Enix Limited.
Unbalance © Tvee Games 2018
Oddmar © Mobge Ltd 2018
FINAL FANTASY XV POCKET EDITION ©
2016, 2018 SQUARE ENIX CO., LTD. All
Rights Reserved
GNOG © KO_OP 2018
Part Time UFO ©2017 HAL Laboratory,
Inc.
Chuchel © Amanita Design 2018
Terraria © 2018 Re-Logic. All rights
reserved.

STAYING SAFE AND HAVING FUN

Always check out a game's rating before you play it. The ratings are there for a reason, not to stop you from having fun. If you're playing online with others, remember that they're not real-life friends. Here are some tips for staying safe when you're gaming online:

1 Talk to your parents about what the rules are in your family about how long you can play games for, what websites you can visit on the Internet, and what you can and can't do.

2 Don't give out your passwords to anyone other than your parents.

3 Don't respond to any conversations that are mean or make you feel bad. It's not your fault if someone sends you something bad. Let your parents know right away.

4 Never agree to meet in person with someone you met online, and never send photographs of yourself or others to anyone you meet online.

5 If you're playing games when you're on the move, be careful and look where you're going.

6 Taking regular breaks when you're gaming is not only good for your eyes—it will also help you get refreshed and improve your play. Don't forget to put your mobile device down every now and then to take a time out.

7 Don't forget—games are meant to be fun! If things aren't going well in the game, just take a break and come back to it later.

8 Don't download or install games or apps to any device, or fill out any forms on the Internet, without first checking with the person that the device you're using belongs to.

9 Don't feel pressured to ever spend any money on games or apps. If a game tells you to spend money, talk to your parents about it.

10 When you're online, be nice to other people. Don't say or do anything that could hurt someone else's feelings or make them feel unhappy.

11 Never give out your personal information such as your real name, phone number, or anything about your parents.

12 Video games are the most amazing things ever! Let everyone know how to have fun playing them, safely.

OLD MAN'S JOURNEY

Stunning-looking environments and an emotional storyline combine to create a charming adventure and one of the standout mobile games of the past year.

CONTENTS

FEATURES

08-17 **THE BEST MOBILE GAMES EVER**
24-31 THE BEST FREE GAMES
34-37 **THE BEST PUZZLE GAMES**
42-43 THE CRAZIEST GAMES
48-51 **THE BEST SPORTS GAMES**
56-57 SHOWCASE: POLY BRIDGE
58-63 **THE BEST INDIE GAMES**
70-71 THE BEST VR GAMES
72-73 **THE BEST AR GAMES**
76-81 THE BEST RETRO GAMES
84-85 **SHOWCASE: MONUMENT VALLEY 2**
86-87 THE HARDEST GAMES
92-93 **THE BEST MULTIPLAYER GAMES**
98-99 THE BEST BRAIN GAMES
104-107 **ESSENTIAL ACCESSORIES**
112-115 THE BEST ESPORT GAMES
120-121 **SHOWCASE: CHUCHEL**
122-123 THE BEST CROSS-PLATFORM GAMES
126-127 **GLOSSARY**

GAMES

18-19 **MINECRAFT**
20 DRAGON BALL LEGENDS
21 **HOLEDOWN**
22 HELLO NEIGHBOR
23 **ODDMAR**
32 ALTO'S ODYSSEY
33 **MONUMENT VALLEY 2**
38-39 FORTNITE
40 **WORLD OF DEMONS**
41 ARKANOID
 VS SPACE INVADERS
44 **OLD MAN'S JOURNEY**
45 SCRIBBLENAUTS UNLIMITED
46 **CLASH ROYALE**
47 DANDARA

52 **ANIMAL CROSSING: POCKET CAMP**

53 VAINGLORY 5V5

54-55 ROBLOX

64 TERRARIA

65 ALPHABEAR 2

66 PART TIME UFO

67 OCMO

68 GNOG

69 LINELIGHT

74 HEARTHSTONE

75 OCEANHORN 2: KNIGHTS OF THE LOST REALM

82 JUST DANCE NOW

83 POKÉMON GO

88-89 FINAL FANTASY XV: POCKET EDITION

90 ASPHALT 9: LEGENDS

91 THE BATTLE OF POLYTOPIA

94 LARA CROFT GO

95 RAYMAN ADVENTURES

96 CHUCHEL

97 POCKET CITY

100 THE SIMS MOBILE

101 SUPERBROTHERS: SWORD & SWORCERY EP

102 DRAGON HILLS 2

103 MORPHITE

108 COMMAND & CONQUER: RIVALS

109 SILLY WALKS

110 SPLITTER CRITTERS

111 SPACE PIONEER

116 DISNEY HEROES: BATTLE MODE

117 RUNESCAPE

118 THE ELDER SCROLLS: LEGENDS

119 POLY BRIDGE

124 FROST

125 VIKINGS: AN ARCHER'S JOURNEY

54

88

18

64

WELCOME TO

GO

31

GAMING!

81

Mobile gaming is bigger and better than ever before. Whether you're a keen gamer or a casual player, someone who loves to immerse themselves in a game or simply pick up and play, there's something to keep everyone entertained.

Not only will you find awesome adventures, fast-paced action games, mind-boggling puzzlers, and retro-style platformers, but you can now play the biggest PC and console game in the world on your smartphone. That's right—*Fortnite: Battle Royale* is available in all its glory in the palm of your hand. And that's not all! You can also enjoy other cross-platform favorites—such as *Minecraft* and *Roblox*—while you're on the go.

But it's not just about the big names. The beauty of mobile gaming is that some of the very best games come from the smallest studios. *Monument Valley 2*, *Old Man's Journey*, and *Holedown* are just three of the many incredible indie games we love, and there are even more to discover inside.

In *Go Gaming!* we've put together a collection of the very best games your mobile devices have to offer, featuring tips, tricks, expert advice, and much more! You'll find hundreds of new games to pick up and play, as well as fascinating facts about games you already know and love.

38

22

THE BEST MOBILE GAMES EVER

PACKING YOUR PHONE WITH PERFECTION

There's never been a better time to be gaming on mobile. Exciting action games, brain-teasing puzzlers, superb strategy titles, perfect platformers: mobile has it all. We've picked out the best games you can download right now, including all the coolest new titles and a few classics that just never get old.

40 BAD PIGGIES

This *Angry Birds* spinoff has been around a while, but it's still a fantastic game. In each level of this physics-based puzzler you must get a pig safely from a start point to an end point. You do that by building a crazy contraption for them to ride, made from objects like wheels, umbrellas, balloons, ropes, bottles, and rockets.

39 DIG DOG – TREASURE HUNTER

In this speedy arcade-style game you play as a dog searching for a bone. In each level you've got to quickly dig down to find the bone, while avoiding the monsters walking around and running from the bats that will be chasing you.

38 FINAL FANTASY XV: POCKET EDITION

This entry in the legendary RPG series that is *Final Fantasy* is made especially for mobile, with simple controls and a cool cartoony art style. You battle against monsters with a team of friends and follow an epic story through ten chapters.

37 SLITHER.IO

You control a worm on a screen filled with worms controlled by other players. A worm explodes if its head touches one of the other worms. Worms then eat up the pieces to grow bigger. Your job is to try and block off other players so you can eat up those delicious pieces, but also be very careful someone else doesn't do the same to you.

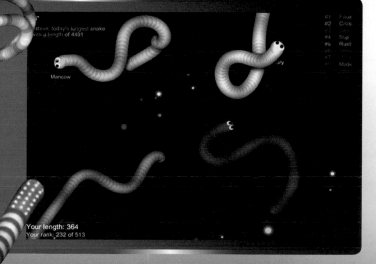

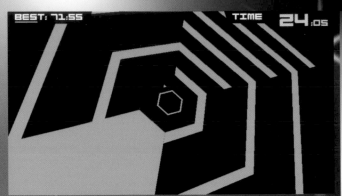

35 PUMPED BMX 3

In this cool BMX game you ride along tracks performing huge jumps and pulling off awesome tricks. There's a fantastic variety of stages and challenges and it feels great every time you complete one.

36 SUPER HEXAGON

If you like your video games super hard then *Super Hexagon* is the game for you. You control a triangle in the middle of the screen that you have to pilot through the gaps in the walls heading toward you. You won't last long on your first go, but keep trying.

34 RAYMAN ADVENTURES

This game is one of the best-looking and best-sounding you can get on mobile, but it's not just great to look at, *Rayman Adventures* is a lot of fun to play, too. Rayman runs through each level at full-speed and you've got to time your jumps to leap over gaps and stomp on bad guys as you save friendly incrediballs that give you special abilities to help you complete each level.

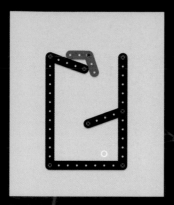

31 ARKANOID VS SPACE INVADERS

This is a mash-up of two gaming classics. There's the ball-bouncing, block-breaking fun of *Arkanoid* and the alien-shooting action of *Space Invaders*. It turns out that these two legends fit together perfectly.

33 ZIP-ZAP

In this game, touching the screen will make the mechanical pieces you control contract and taking your finger off the screen will release them. Using these simple controls you must get the pieces into the right place on the screen to complete over 100 cleverly designed levels.

32 THE WITNESS

In *The Witness* you explore a beautiful island full of line maze puzzle panels for you to discover and solve. They start off easy, but new symbols are gradually added to make them harder. The cool thing is there are no instructions telling you what the symbols mean, so it's down to you to figure it out. That moment when a puzzle clicks in your head and you realize how it works feels amazing.

29 LUMINO CITY

Everything you see in *Lumino City* is real, handmade and then photographed to appear in the game. You get to explore this amazing hand-crafted world and solve puzzles as you go. Each puzzle is different, so you never know what you will discover next.

30 LINELIGHT

In *Linelight* you must guide a little light through levels made only of lines. New ideas are added as you go. Each is simple enough that you can understand it instantly, but as ideas are combined and used in more complicated settings, *Linelight* really starts to give your brain a workout.

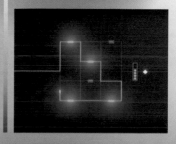

28 80 DAYS

Can you make it around the world in 80 days? That's the challenge in front of you in this story-based adventure. You must make choices on every step of your journey that impact on your story and your chances of achieving your goal.

26 IT'S FULL OF SPARKS

The fuse on your firecracker is burning down and you've got to beat the level before it runs out. That makes this platformer a race against time, forcing you to run, jump, and dodge at full speed to make it to the end.

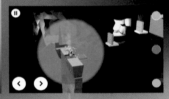

27 RIDICULOUS FISHING

You cast your line into the water and must try and dodge fish as your hook sinks. On the way up you've got to guide it into as many fish as possible to catch them. With the cash you earn from your catches you can upgrade your rod so that you can catch even more.

25 WORLD OF GOO

World of Goo is one of the first great mobile games, and it still holds up today. In each level you use goo balls to build towers, bridges, and other structures to make a path for your goo balls over gaps, hills, and other obstacles to get safely to the level's exit.

24 CANDY CRUSH SAGA

There are lots of match-three puzzle games on mobile, but none as big as the megahit that is *Candy Crush Saga*. You have to swap colored pieces of candy around on a board to try and match up at least three of the same color and take them out of the game.

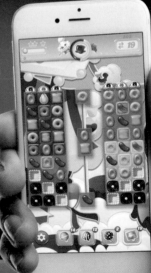

21 PROJECT HIGHRISE

Project Highrise is a game where you must build and manage a skyscraper. You've got to think about everything, from wiring to the happiness of your tenants. Keeping your skyscraper running smoothly while still making money is a tough job.

23 YOU MUST BUILD A BOAT

The goal of the game is there in the title: you must build a boat. You do this by going into dungeons to battle monsters and find resources in the form of a match-three puzzle game. You can use what you find to upgrade your boat and abilities for the next run.

20 HERO ACADEMY 2

Hero Academy 2 is part card game and part strategy game. You collect cards with different heroes and abilities on them to build a deck and then use your cards in turn-based battles against other players. You need to think carefully about both sides of the game to be successful.

19 FINGER DRIVER

This game is exactly what it sounds like from the title. You put your finger on the screen to take control of a steering wheel and weave a speeding car around exciting race tracks. It's a smooth, simple, and satisfying racer that's perfect for mobile.

22 CLASH OF CLANS

In *Clash of Clans* you are the chief of a village. By attacking the villages of other players you can earn gold to build up your own village. You can also join clans made of up to 50 people and take part in big clan war battles.

17 PART TIME UFO

Part arcade crane game simulator and part puzzle game, you progress by stacking and balancing a host of bizarre things as odd jobs to earn cash for your new life on Earth. Cute, charming, and a real challenge.

18 THE SIMS FREEPLAY

You get to build your own house and take control of your own customized Sims in this great mobile entry to *The Sims* series. There are 55 levels to play through to unlock new content.

16 ODDMAR

Take control of the Viking Oddmar and guide him on an epic journey through forests, mountains, and mines on his quest to prove himself a true Viking. It's a fantastic platformer full of enemies to battle and even a few physics-based puzzles for you to solve.

15 SUPER MARIO RUN

Unlike most *Mario* games, Mario runs by himself in *Super Mario Run*. Your job is to time his jumps to avoid hazards, stomp on Goombas, and collect as many coins as you can on your way to the end of each level.

14 SUZY CUBE

Suzy Cube is a cute and colorful 3-D platformer. Your goal is to recover the gold stolen from Castle Cubeton by the evil Skulls. There are over 40 stages to beat, cool power-ups to use, and secrets to discover.

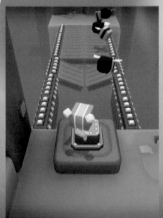

13 OVIVO

In this super-stylish platformer you control a little blob that can change color. When your blob is black it will stand on black, but when you switch to white it will slip through and hang upside down as if attached to a ceiling. One of the coolest things is the way you can build up speed by falling and then switch colors to start throwing yourself in the other direction.

12 FLIPPING LEGEND

In this fun, fast-paced arcade adventure you tap to flip your character between tiles and move forward on a patterned grid. You've got to have great reflexes to take out enemies and avoid hazards to get as far as you can and unlock new characters to play with.

11 KALIMBA

You control two colored pieces of totem pole at the same time and must get them to avoid trouble, hit switches, and generally work together to get through each stage. The game is always introducing clever new ideas to keep things interesting.

10 CRASHLANDS

At the beginning of this fantastic adventure exploration game your character crash-lands on a planet. You've got to scavenge for resources, fight and tame monsters, craft new items, complete quests, build up your base, and more in your quest to call for help and get rescued.

9 HIDDEN FOLKS

Hidden Folks is like an interactive *Where's Waldo?*. Each of its hand-drawn environments is like a little 2-D toy box for you to poke around in to try and find the characters that are hiding there. The level of detail is mind-blowing and makes exploring each scene to see what you can discover loads of fun.

8 METEORFALL: JOURNEY

 You can choose from one of four hero cards at the beginning of *Meteorfall*. By defeating enemies, you collect more cards to add to your deck and help you battle your way to defeat the final boss, Uberlich.

5 ALTO'S ODYSSEY

 Snowboard your way through beautiful desert landscapes in a game that's somehow as relaxing as it is challenging. You can pull off massive jumps and cool tricks across stunning scenery to boost your score and unlock new upgrades to help you get farther the next time you play.

7 THREES!

3 In *Threes!* you start by matching up 1s to make 2s, then 1s and 2s to make 3s. From there you can only match up multiples of three—6, 12, and so on—as you chase the highest score possible.

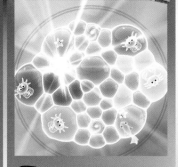

$1 + 2 = 3$

6 TINY BUBBLES

 In this bubbly puzzle game you pop, inflate, and match colored bubbles by breaking the edges between them. You must plan ahead to match colors and think about the little critters that will sometimes be inside the bubbles to meet the goals.

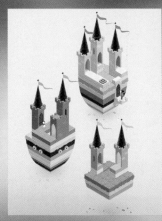

4 MONUMENT VALLEY 2

The sequel to another great mobile title, this perspective-bending puzzle game is full of delightful surprises. Twisting and playing with the levels reveals new routes for your character to walk down in your quest to get through each of the game's beautiful puzzle-box stages.

3 POKÉMON GO

Pokémon GO is a great way of combining video game adventures with real ones. As you walk around in the real world Pokémon will appear on your phone for you to catch, level up, and evolve. You can then send them to battle in gyms to try and take them for your chosen team.

2 FORTNITE

You get dropped from the sky at the beginning of each match in *Fortnite* and must look for weapons, items, and resources to build fortifications as soon as you land. The safe zone gradually gets smaller as the game goes on, forcing you and up to 100 other players into a battle to be the last one standing.

EXPERT COMMENT
JOHN RIBBINS

Co-founder of Roll7, developers of *Laser League* and *OlliOlli2*

I've always been a huge fan of Arnold Rauers' games—*Miracle Merchant* and *Card Thief*. They both have super nice art styles and are simple (but super fun) card games based around making magic potions or sneaking into dingy castles. I don't like my mobile games to be too fast-paced or twitchy, something turn-based where I can take my time is my preference. For me they're the perfect dip-in, dip-out games for sitting on the train, but I can also lose a whole evening on them just slouched on the couch!

1 MINECRAFT: POCKET EDITION

The thing that makes *Minecraft* such a great game is that you can choose your own experience. You can build huge castles or riverside cottages, go adventuring in monster-filled mines and alternative dimensions, farm food, craft awesome armor, brew potions, raise animals, build trains, and so much more. The incredible number of options, freedom to focus on whatever you want, and the game's huge randomly generated worlds mean *Minecraft* can feel new, exciting, and different every time you pick it up.

FAST FACT

The first version of the megahit that is *Minecraft* was created by developer Markus Persson in only six days. It has now sold over 144 million copies across all platforms worldwide.

The *Minecraft* store has lots of customized worlds, including medieval castles, Western saloons, and even a world with dinosaurs.

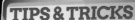

MINECRAFT
CREATE YOUR VERY OWN WORLDS

Anyone who has so much as looked at a games console, tablet, or phone knows what *Minecraft* is. That blocky bundle of joy has pretty much taken over the world and it's easy to see why. Where else can you create your very own living, breathing worlds? And yet, *Minecraft* isn't just about building. It's about working with friends to overcome a challenge or venturing into unknown lands in search of loot. And since the "Better Together Update," players can now play on servers, meaning the possibilities are truly endless.

TIPS & TRICKS

FOOD SUPPLY
Animals are the best source of food when you load up a new world. Grab cobblestone and wood and get cooking!

HOW TO BEAT SKELETONS
Just build a three-high spike and when they start attacking, wait for them to come to you, then start swinging.

DON'T DIG STRAIGHT DOWN
Build a two-wide shaft and mine up each tile while standing on the opposite block. It's the best way to avoid falling in lava.

LIKE THIS? ALSO CHECK OUT...

TERRARIA
Imagine *Minecraft* viewed from the side. *Terraria* is a 2-D side-scrolling builder including action-adventure. Build, survive, explore—like *Minecraft* meets *Mario*.

ROBLOX
With 70 million active users, *Roblox* is similar to *Minecraft*, but with a larger focus on user-generated content (UGC). Want new game modes or custom skins? Then why not create them yourself!

TOP 5... HOUSES TO BUILD WHEN YOU FIRST SPAWN

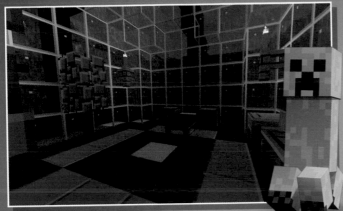

UNDERWATER HOUSE

1 Creepers can't blow stuff up in water. Therefore, underwater homes are a lot safer than creating builds above land. For this all you need is a simple five-wide dome made from glass, blocks to cover the water inside, a sign, and a host of the usual useful appliances.

STANDARD VILLAGER HOUSE

2 The villager house doesn't get enough credit. It's easy to build, offers protection, and has just enough space for a chest, crafting table, and a double bed. And it's only five-by-five blocks in diameter. You can build it by chopping down just two trees!

SANDY MOUND

3 Much like building into a mountain, building underground also offers safety. Plop a door down, surround with sand, then build steps leading to your underground bunker. With enough torches dotted about, there's no reason a mob would spawn and follow you down there at night.

FAST FACT

Each month, *Minecraft* is played by 74 million people—more people than there are in California and Texas combined. It's sold more than 144 million copies, over twice the amount of people in the UK.

BUILD INTO A MOUNTAIN

4 When you first spawn, you'll be in a mad dash for resources. Rather than waste all your wood building a small house, save that wood for cooking and build a house directly into the side of a mountain. All you need are some doors and a pickax and you're good to go.

SKY HOUSE

5 Where's the safest place in a survival world? That's easy. It's in the sky. Mobs can't reach you and you've still got enough sun to allow crops to grow. But how would you get to a sky house? Just dump some water coming off the side and ride the waterfall up and down.

It wouldn't be *Dragon Ball* if you couldn't unleash Goku's signature Kamehameha. Using your skill cards you have many other special moves at your disposal.

FAST FACT

Protagonist Shallot is a brand-new character in the *Dragon Ball* universe, personally designed by series creator Akira Toriyama.

TIPS & TRICKS

UNLOCKING CHARACTERS
You'll need to summon new characters via a randomized system. Story events will also reward you with new characters.

MASTERING THE ELEMENTS
Color-coded elements will determine what each character is strong or weak against. Use this to your advantage.

VANISHING ACT
Swipe left or right to dodge enemy attacks and give yourself the chance to counter. There's a meter, so use it wisely.

DRAGON BALL LEGENDS

ANIME ON THE GO(KU)

Dragon Ball fans, rejoice. A new Tournament of Time brings legendary heroes from across time as they fight three-on-three battles to determine who's the strongest. Assemble Goku and the gang as you swipe and tap with your finger in beautiful 3-D battles in real-time! With the power of arts cards you'll be able to unleash Super Saiyan moves! With a story mode and the ability to challenge other players across the world, this is the ultimate *Dragon Ball* game in the palm of your hand.

LIKE THIS? ALSO CHECK OUT...

MARVEL STRIKE FORCE
If you're not interested in anime, how about assembling your own Avengers in this turn-based role-playing game instead? Features superheroes and supervillains, as well as the agents of SHIELD.

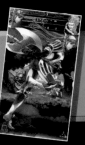

FIRE EMBLEM HEROES
Nintendo's beloved tactical role-playing series also pulls characters from across timelines to do battle on palm-sized maps. *Fire Emblem*'s signature weapon triangle system transfers to mobile, too.

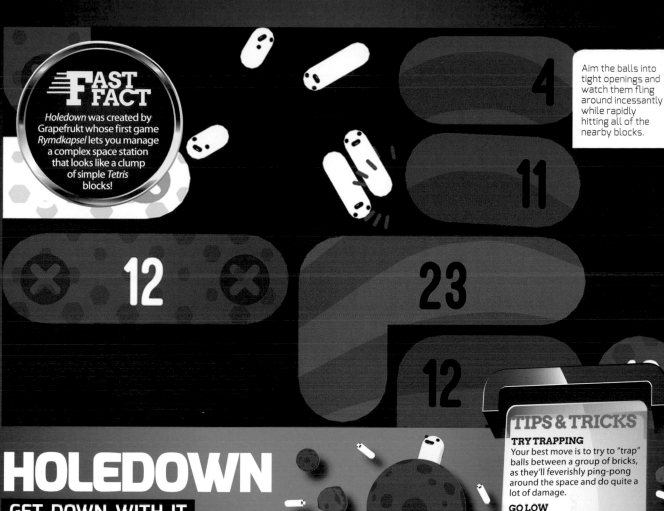

FAST FACT

Holedown was created by Grapefrukt whose first game *Rymdkapsel* lets you manage a complex space station that looks like a clump of simple *Tetris* blocks!

Aim the balls into tight openings and watch them fling around incessantly while rapidly hitting all of the nearby blocks.

HOLEDOWN

GET DOWN WITH IT

oledown puts a fun twist on brick-breaker games: instead of hitting a ball to smash floating bricks above, you simply fire a ball down into ever-deepening holes to clear colorful blocks. Each block must be hit a certain number of times before it's cleared, and you'll need to remove them before they reach the top line to end your game. Success depends on both smart aiming and lucky bounces, along with a steady stream of upgrades—like one that eventually lets you fire 99 balls at once. That's handy!

TIPS & TRICKS

TRY TRAPPING
Your best move is to try to "trap" balls between a group of bricks, as they'll feverishly ping-pong around the space and do quite a lot of damage.

GO LOW
Resist the urge to always clear the top blocks first: eliminating lower ones will cause any non-locked upper blocks (that they're supporting) to fall away.

UPGRADE WISELY
The "Ball Buffer" upgrade is hugely helpful, as it boosts your maximum ball count, while the "Hold Size" upgrade lets you snag more upgrade crystals in each session.

LIKE THIS? ALSO CHECK OUT…

TWOFOLD INC.
Twofold Inc. was the previous game by the creator of *Holedown* and it boasts a similarly minimal look, but with a different kind of game. Here you'll create chains of like-colored blocks to clear them from the screen, while also meeting various demands.

ARKANOID VS SPACE INVADERS
This fast and frenzied game combines the retro brick-breaker design of *Arkanoid* with the pixel aliens from gaming classic *Space Invaders*. It's a clever and fun combo.

Hello Neighbor can now fit in your pocket! The game is fun to play on a small screen, and it gets even spookier if you play it under a blanket at night.

F AST FACT

Secret Neighbor is an upcoming multiplayer game, in which you and your friends sneak into the neighbor's house to rescue a friend. The only problem is one of the players is a traitor in disguise.

HELLO NEIGHBOR

HE'S COMING TO GET YOU . . .

Get ready for the most twisted, bizarre game of hide-and-seek ever! In *Hello Neighbor* you have to sneak into your shady neighbor's house to find the secrets within. But he's not happy with your snooping, so he hunts you down, forcing you to hide and throw him off your path. Things get so tense it almost feels like you're trapped in a scary movie!

TIPS & TRICKS

ALWAYS PLAN AN ESCAPE
When you're exploring the house, look for an escape route first and try not to back yourself into a corner. That way, you can run from danger.

HIDE OFTEN
Hiding is part of staying safe and you should make it a habit to hide until danger passes.

SEE WHAT WORKS
Experiment with different tactics to see how the neighbor reacts. Sometimes the solution isn't the most obvious.

LIKE THIS? ALSO CHECK OUT...

COUNTERSPY
In this side-scrolling game, you have to try and keep two warring countries in check as an agent of C.O.U.N.T.E.R. The emphasis is on stealth and quick reactions.

COWARD KNIGHT
Don't be fooled by its cute looks: this top-down stealth game is very difficult. You must save the princess as you play the last remaining knight. For those after a serious challenge only!

ODDMAR
THE LITTLE VIKING THAT COULD

It's true—Oddmar isn't the most popular Viking in his village. He eats too much and doesn't do his fair share of work. So to prove himself, Oddmar sets off into the forest to help his people and earn himself a special place in Valhalla. Slice and dice your way through 24 hand-drawn levels with upgradable weapons and a surfable shield. Good thing you're not alone on this epic quest: you can ride a wild boar and even take control of a giant flying squirrel!

TIPS & TRICKS

SHOP 'TIL YOU DROP
Stop at all the different stores to upgrade your weapon and shield. This means you can increase those Viking powers!

UNDER THE BRIDGE
During the troll chase, keep running right while avoiding the beast's slamming attacks. Time jumps as the platforms fall.

ROCK AND ROLL
Golem boss: dodge the red rocks, platforms, and charge attacks until a blue vial falls. Knock it into the rock monster to strike.

FAST FACT
Oddmar is based on several fun characters from Norse mythology. Both the Kraken (a giant squid) and Loki (a shape-shifting trickster god) show up during this exciting 2-D adventure.

LIKE THIS? ALSO CHECK OUT...

STAR KNIGHT
One of the more difficult mobile games available, this challenging 2-D action-platformer features moody shadow graphics, a mysterious hero, and a huge sword.

DAN THE MAN
Fancy something a little retro? This old-school platformer has you punching, kicking, and exploding your way through tons of chaotic stages. It's like playing in an action movie.

THE BEST FREE GAMES

HAVING FUN FOR FREE

One of the things we love about mobile is how many games there are out there that you can play for free. As long as you're careful to avoid in-app purchases and don't mind seeing the odd ad, there's no reason why you can't get hours of fun without paying a single cent. If anyone thought that free games can't be as good as paid ones, then here are some amazing titles to prove them wrong.

SUPER MONKEY BALL: SAKURA

Control the rolling monkey by tilting your mobile device so that the little guy rolls in the direction you're aiming for. Each stage has a time limit so you have to be quick without messing up!

ORBIA

Tap on the white circles to make your character fly to them, but you have to be careful to avoid the spinning enemies that can block you off.

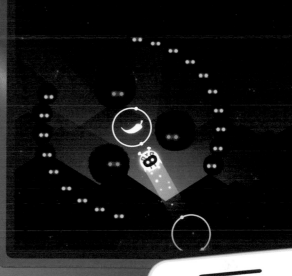

PSYCH!

This fun party game asks you to invent fake answers to trivia questions. Other players do the same. You then try and guess the correct answer without getting tricked by one of the fake ones and giving away points.

DISC DRIVIN' 2

Compete against friends as you take turns flicking discs around a track. Master your technique to get your disc sweeping around curves and avoiding hazards in the least amount of moves possible.

RIDER

Simply press down on your screen and the motorcycle that you control in *Rider* will start speeding up. While in the air, holding the screen will make your cycle perform flips. You can speed around tricky courses, but you have to clear huge jumps and pull off crazy stunts to survive.

UP GOLF

 In this fun arcade-inspired golf game, you choose an animal pal and hit them upward like a golf ball as the screen gradually scrolls up in never-ending levels. It's fun to compete against friends' scores and see which of you can get the highest.

THE BATTLE OF POLYTOPIA

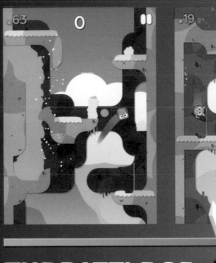 In *The Battle of Polytopia*, you explore automatically generated worlds, build cities, research new technologies, and take over the land in this fast-paced take on the civilization building game genre.

WORDS WITH FRIENDS 2

 **In this *Scrabble*-inspired word game, you can play against friends online to achieve the highest-scoring words possible on each turn. You can take part in multiple games at the same time, which means you don't have to spend ages waiting for other players to take their turn.**

BALLZ

 Your objective in this game is to take out as many bricks as possible by swiping to throw balls. The screen will keep scrolling to reveal new bricks. As the bricks appear, flick your ball directly at them to boost your score.

COOKING FEVER

Manage your time carefully to prepare delicious gourmet dishes. Using over 100 ingredients, a host of kitchen appliances, and a variety of different restaurants, you'll have plenty of challenges to juggle and meals to cook. Bon appétit!

EGG, INC.

Can you build an empire out of eggs? In this game you can! Using the money you earn from selling eggs, you can build hen houses, hire new drivers, and unlock new tech to improve productivity and get the cash rolling in. Discovering whether the chicken or egg came first was never so much fun!

TIMBERMAN

Your character will chop wood at a crazy pace, bringing branches racing down toward you. You have to swap sides to avoid the descending branches and to make sure you keep your lumberjack busy chopping.

CUT THE ROPE: MAGIC

Simply slide your finger across the screen to cut the ropes attached to a cute character and the candy he wants. Just make sure you cut the correct ropes! Unlike previous editions of *Cut the Rope*, this one lets you change your character.

FINAL FANTASY BRAVE EXVIUS

FFBE challenges you to fight battles with characters from across *Final Fantasy*'s legendary RPG series. Each win earns points for materials and cash.

DOES NOT COMMUTE

You start this game by driving a car from point A to point B. Simple, right? However, when you drive the next car, the journey that the first car took will play out again, and so on, and so on. Eventually your screen will be filled with the chaos of your previous journeys and you'll need great reactions and driving skills to weave around a city that becomes continually more crowded.

POCKET RUN POOL

Pool is a game where you have to plan your shots ahead—but even more so in this game. Score multipliers rotate around each pocket every time you pot a ball, so you have to think about where the multipliers will be next to achieve the highest score possible.

SKY FORCE RELOADED

In this intense top-down shoot 'em up, you have to move your spaceship around the screen while avoiding enemies, blasting their ships into pieces, and fighting massive screen-filling bosses. There are a variety of different ships to pilot and upgrade with new weapons and shields.

PINOUT!

The objective in this pinball game is to remove as many bricks as you can to propel the ball as far as possible. The screen will keep scrolling to reveal new bricks and you must flick your ball to break them in order to boost your score.

ASPHALT 8: AIRBORNE

Asphalt has some of its best racing games on the mobile format and *Asphalt 8* is no exception. Customize your vehicles and take them out to speed around tracks from all around the world: Tokyo, Dubai, the Nevada desert, and more.

AMAZING KATAMARI DAMACY

Roll an ever-growing ball that picks up every object in its path to swell to epic proportions in this runner from the *Katamari* series.

TRIALS FRONTIER

Ride a motorcycle over tough tracks, carefully balancing your bike by shifting your weight backward and forward like a professional. Wheelie your way over obstacles, land huge jumps, and pull off massive stunts. It's not an easy game, but it's very satisfying when you perfectly nail a level.

SUPER STICKMAN GOLF 3

There's no other way to describe *Super Stickman Golf 3* than just to say it's a fantastic golf game. Line up your shots, get the power and spin right, and swipe your way through the crazy courses. It features power-ups, collectible cards, and a multiplayer mode.

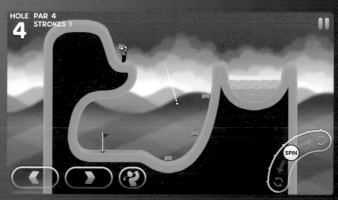

ALPHABEAR

Alphabear adds a few cool twists to the *Scrabble*-style word game. Using tiles unlocks other tiles next to them, but if you don't use them for a number of turns, they'll turn to stone. You can choose a team of three bears with different bonuses to help you in each game.

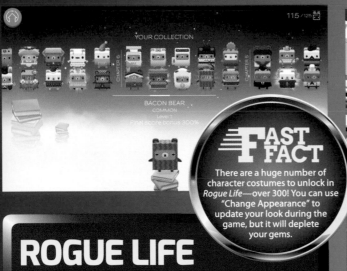

CROSSY ROAD

In *Crossy Road*, you must hop your way across busy roads full of traffic, over floating logs running down rivers, and other dangerous obstacles. The game goes on forever, so it's about lasting as long as you can to gain high scores and unlock new characters.

FAST FACT

There are a huge number of character costumes to unlock in *Rogue Life*—over 300! You can use "Change Appearance" to update your look during the game, but it will deplete your gems.

ROGUE LIFE

You're going to need quick reactions to be successful in *Rogue Life*. Enemies will be firing at you all the time, so you need to be able to dodge quickly while firing back. Recruit new characters with different abilities onto your team and put them to work crafting new tools to help you in battle.

THE SIMS FREEPLAY

In this free version of EA's popular life simulation series, you build houses and control virtual people called Sims. You can design their dream home, decide how your Sim interacts with other Sims in the town, and complete quests to progress through the game.

ANIMAL CROSSING: POCKET CAMP

Be a campsite manager in the relaxing sim that is *Animal Crossing: Pocket Camp*. Help the animals by collecting fruit, catching bugs, or going fishing. Craft items and build the site to suit your style.

ANGRY BIRDS 2

A long time mobile favorite, *Angry Birds* is still as much fun as ever. Pull back a sling loaded with your feathered friends and fire 'em at the constructions where bad piggies are hiding to knock them all down. The fewer shots you can do it in, the better the rating you'll get.

CLASH ROYALE

For *Clash Royale* success, collect a powerful deck of cards with a good mix of troops, spells, and defenses. Then use them to protect your towers and try to knock down your enemies in a tower defense match.

SUPER MARIO RUN

The king of video game platforming has finally made his way to mobile—great news for anyone who loves gaming on the go. Unlike traditional games featuring Mario and his pals, the plumber runs forward by himself in *Super Mario Run*, leaving it up to you to time his jumps to safely complete each level while collecting as many coins as possible. Grabbing the special colored coins will unlock new ones the next time you play through, offering you a new challenge when you replay levels you've already finished. There are a variety of characters from the Mario series to unlock, too, including Princess Peach, Luigi, and Yoshi.

FAST FACT

Nintendo recently revealed that its popular one-handed game, *Super Mario Run*, was partly inspired by speedrunners who never let go of "forward" when they are playing *Mario* games.

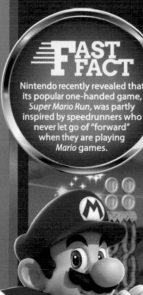

ALTO'S ODYSSEY

EVERY SNOWBOARDER'S DREAM

This might be the most relaxing game you'll ever play. In *Alto's Odyssey*, you play as Alto, who flows through sand dunes and ruins on his trusty snowboard. Although you can grind telephone wires and slide along walls for points, that's not the real aim of this adventure. The fun part is becoming absorbed in this gorgeous world of sunsets and rainstorms. Gaze at the stylish graphics as you sweep through the world on your 'board. It's poetry in motion: It's art come to life. One of the most beautiful games you'll ever play.

TIPS & TRICKS

NO DISTRACTIONS
Turn off the TV. Put your phone on silent. Switch off background music. The key to enjoying *Alto's Odyssey* is to flow through the game without any distractions.

BACKFLIP FOR POINTS
Tap the screen to jump and hold your finger on the screen to backflip. Get into the habit of backflipping when pulling off large jumps to squeeze out extra points.

WALL-RIDE WHEN POSSIBLE
Look for walls with dots on. You can wall-ride these to score extra points and extend your combo further. They're the key to smashing those high-score records.

FAST FACT

Created by indie developer Snowman, *Alto's Odyssey* is the sequel to 2015 breakout hit, *Alto's Adventure*, which features the same mesmerizing art style.

The key is to relax while playing *Alto's Odyssey* and try to feel the "flow" of each level. It's how the game creators made each level.

LIKE THIS? ALSO CHECK OUT…

JETPACK JOYRIDE
One of the biggest and best endless runner games out there. The action quickly becomes chaotic, so this is only recommended for those gamers who have nerves of steel!

SMASH HIT
For an endless runner with a bit of a difference, try your hand at *Smash Hit*. This game takes place in first-person rather than from the side of the screen, giving the action an intense twist.

MONUMENT VALLEY 2

LIKE MOTHER, LIKE DAUGHTER

fter the critical and commercial success of the first game, who can resist another trip to *Monument Valley* with more exquisite and frustrating architectural puzzles to solve?

This time, you're not alone. With more of a story to follow, you play as Ro, whose daughter also follows her on this adventure as they learn to navigate illusionary paths, manipulate surroundings, and learn of its mysteries together.

Whether or not you've played the original version, it's a delightful journey with some breathtaking artistry that is made from the stuff of dreams.

FAST FACT

The parent-child story was influenced by the developers, many of whom had become parents since the first *Monument Valley* game was made.

TIPS & TRICKS

MOVING MOUNTAINS
You can control your characters with a tap but some puzzles also require manipulating the environment. Investigate what you can slide, rotate, or pull apart.

A NEW PERSPECTIVE
Solving puzzles for these isometric levels requires a shift in your perspective. What may look like an inaccessible path is suddenly made possible.

CHILD'S PLAY
Having another character with you changes gameplay dynamics as you need to move Ro's daughter onto certain blocks. They even get separated at certain levels!

As well as the fantastically designed architecture, you'll also meet new friends, like the Totem, made up of blocks stacked on top of one another.

LIKE THIS? ALSO CHECK OUT...

LUMINO CITY
A puzzle adventure where you explore beautiful worlds hand-crafted in paper and card. As well as being a tactile wonder, there's also a story to be told as you race to rescue your kidnapped grandfather.

WONDERPUTT
Miniature golf played across 18 wonderfully designed dioramas. With easy touch-and-drag controls, it's a relaxing and unique take on the game, though there are also leaderboards to keep it competitive.

THE BEST PUZZLE GAMES

PICKING OUR WAY TO PUZZLE PERFECTION

We love the way these games make you feel when you find the solution to a tricky puzzle. Sure, they can be frustrating when you get stuck, but it's all worth it when a puzzle finally clicks in your mind and you feel like a genius! From detective mysteries and physics-based bridge building to brain-teasing word games and colorful shape-swappers, we pick out some of the best puzzle games you can play on mobile right now.

EUCLIDEAN LANDS

Imagine a game where the board is a Rubik's Cube and you'll start to get an idea of what this game is all about. You control a character on the board that can move one space at a time, but you can also twist cubes on each stage to change the level itself!

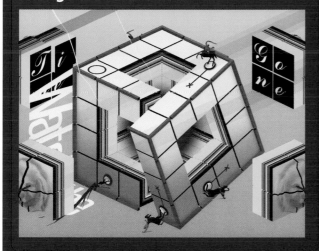

BRIDGE CONSTRUCTOR PORTAL

This game is a cool mix of puzzle ideas. You build bridges to get your test cars from the beginning to the end of levels, avoiding hazards on the way. You can also use portals that will teleport cars from one part of the stage to another. Ensuring your bridges are strong enough to hold the required weight, avoiding the traps and pitfalls that could wreck your cars, and planning ahead so cars don't smash into each other while they're teleporting can be a real juggling act.

FAST FACT

The two separate games *Bridge Constructor* and *Portal* combined to create this game, which will appeal to those who are interested in engineering and construction, as well as puzzles!

CAUSALITY

In *Causality*, you must guide a group of stranded astronauts to safety. Each stage starts with the astronauts running into trouble, but by rewinding time and swapping things around, you can make sure they get safely to the exit. The features make this game a lot of fun.

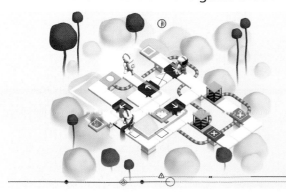

TYPESHIFT

This clever word game is a mix of various word-related games: anagrams, word searches, and a touch of regular crosswords. You are given a series of jumbled-up letters that are organized in columns and you must shift them up and down to try and find the words that are hidden within. Find key words to solve the word puzzles quicker.

FROST

In this relaxing minimalist puzzle game ideally suited to playing on phones, your goal is to guide a swarm of color to an orb that matches its color. It's easy at first, but as the game goes on, you start having to mix swarms together to get the right color, avoid hazards, and so on. Great to both play and watch.

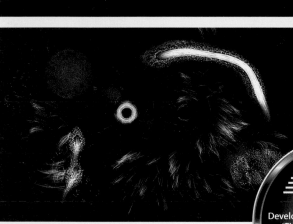

MINESWEEPER GENIUS

This smart little puzzler adds a cool new twist to the classic game *Minesweeper*. As with the original version, you use the numbers on the screen to figure out which of the tiles are hiding bombs. Once you've figured that out, you can guide your cute character on a safe path through the level.

FAST FACT

Developed by Mother Gaia Studio (*Tiny Empire*, *Tank Invaders*), *Minesweeper Genius* features a built-in AI that ensures each level it creates is beatable before it is presented to the player.

SPLITTER CRITTERS

It may look cute and cuddly, but *Splitter Critters* is full of tricky puzzles. The idea behind the game is that you can make cuts in the level to split it up into different pieces and then slide them around to make a safe path for the cute critters to get to their spaceship.

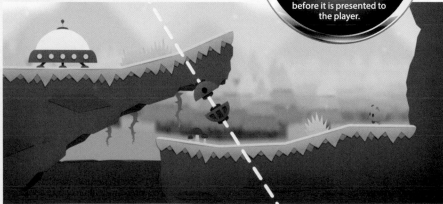

WORDSCAPES

 In *Wordscapes*, you need to find and sketch out words from a group of letters displayed on your screen in a circle. Find one of the right words and that word will then appear in the crossword-style grid above it. It's a great mix of quick-thinking, spelling skill, and testing your word knowledge.

FAST FACT

Layton's Mystery Journey is the seventh main entry in the long-running *Professor Layton* puzzle series. Developed by Level-5, it features the young heroine searching for her missing father.

DISSEMBLER

Each puzzle in *Dissembler* is a cool design made of colors wrapped up together. Your task is to take that colorful collection of shapes apart piece by piece by flipping tiles to match colors up and make them disappear. There's something really satisfying about gradually unraveling each puzzle.

LAYTON'S MYSTERY JOURNEY

Playing as detective Katrielle Layton, you travel around London searching for clues and solving puzzles to uncover the truth behind mysteries. The game tells a great story as well as being a fun puzzle game.

FAST FACT

Everything you need to play and win *Fortnite* comes for free as standard, there's no need to spend any money in the game!

FORTNITE
EARN THAT VICTORY ROYALE!

Now you can play *Fortnite* on the go! Battle Royale features the same awesome gameplay, the same map, the same weapons, and, yes, the same regular updates! There's now no excuse for not enjoying this great game whether you're at home or on the move.

It will take some getting used to on the smaller screen as all of the controls have been turned into touch inputs, but once you get used to it you'll find that *Fortnite* is just as much fun to play on mobile!

TIPS & TRICKS

ADJUST YOUR SCREEN SENSITIVITY
If you want cleaner movement and kills, duck into settings and adjust Touch Sensitivity from 40 to 60, then take Touch Scope Sensitivity down to 65.

NEVER STOP BUILDING
Spend time gathering resources and practice building whenever you get a chance.

STICK WITH YOUR FRIENDS
If you are playing in Squad mode try not to wander away from your allies. You need to stick by your friends and cover their backs.

ALSO CHECK OUT…

MINECRAFT: POCKET EDITION
You build pretty much anything you want in *Minecraft*, so why not try and make your own battle royale-style game? Get some friends together, set the rules, and have some fun!

INFINITY BLADE TRILOGY
With its exciting sword-fighting action and immersive storylines, Epic's *Infinity Blade* series is well worth checking out. Winners of the prestigious Apple Design Award and more than 40 other awards!

TOP 5... STRATEGIES

PLAY IT SAFE

1 You don't *have* to jump out of the Battle Bus immediately. Instead, why not try a location a little further down the line, taking the time to gather a few resources and weapons before you wade into the fray. It's the easiest way to guarantee a top 20 finish.

BUILDAHOLIC

2 Touch down in one of the forests adorning the edge of the map and start gathering every single resource you can get your hands on and get to building. The idea here is to construct a variety of towers and structures that look imposing from a distance; it'll help to keep players away from you for a while.

SUPER STEALTHY

3 If you want to play it safe you should attempt to stick as close to the edge of the closing circle as physically possible. Most players will move to the center of it, leaving you free to slowly pick up weapons and items as you go, preparing you for the late-game battle without forcing you into early conflict.

FRENZIED ASSAULT

4 Sometimes you just want to cause a little chaos, right? Jump out of the bus as soon as the prompt comes up on screen and get ready for a frenzied battle as soon as your boots hit the ground. You might not last very long, but you'll sure have a good time!

THE TROLL

5 For this strategy to work you'll need a selection of good weapons and will need to go out in search of enemies. The idea is to draw other players out into the open by goading them before you then disappear into cover— hopefully other enemies will pick them off, leaving you free to keep moving forward.

FAST FACT

World of Demons's distinct art style is inspired by Ukiyo-e, a form of Japanese art commonly produced as woodblock prints.

熊
KUMA DOJI

鬼
ONIMARU

夜
SAYO

WORLD OF DEMONS

GOTTA SLAY 'EM ALL

Set in a fantastical version of feudal Japan taken over by Oni (demons), only the most powerful samurai can fearlessly do battle to save the world. Slash, dodge, and parry your way through intense action against a variety of yokai (monsters based on Japanese folklore). The game includes story Skirmishes, PvP, and co-op to offer variety and challenge. This is an action experience like no other.

TIPS & TRICKS

COMBAT MOVEMENT
While attacks are automatic, your priority is controlling your samurai's movement, swiping the screen to dodge.

YOUR YOKAI
You can also recruit yokai who can confer stat boosts for you in combat. Their strengths are governed by elements.

UPGRADING YOUR ARSENAL
There's a wealth of upgrades and customization available, from increasing your health to new sword skills. Use these to defeat tougher enemies.

LIKE THIS? ALSO CHECK OUT...

HONKAI IMPACT 3RD
An action game with hi-res graphics starring a group of cute but deadly anime girls. Not only is gameplay satisfyingly responsive, there are also lavishly produced cut-scenes.

INFINITY BLADE
A ground-breaking RPG game—known as the first mobile game to run on Unreal Engine—where you fight one-on-one battles against fearsome beasts.

ARKANOID VS SPACE INVADERS

BLASTS FROM THE PAST

Both *Arkanoid* and *Space Invaders* are gaming icons from decades back, but all you really need to know is that this mobile mash-up shows how two great games can work together. *Arkanoid vs Space Invaders* starts with the brick-breaking format of the first game—in which you smack a ball around a stage with a paddle—but you'll bounce back the laser shots that the alien invaders shoot your way. It's a neat twist that keeps the arcade spirit of both classics, yet also creates an entirely new experience for today.

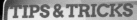

Arkanoid vs Space Invaders' pixel aliens are shooting at you! Defend yourself by moving a large paddle to reflect the shots back at them.

TIPS & TRICKS

POWER UP!
Having trouble with a level? Use your hard-earned coins to buy a special item for an added boost. They can double the ball's strength or extend your paddle, for example.

STRAIGHT SHOOTER
Reflected shots will angle off your paddle, but you can fire them straight back toward the bricks by swiping up toward them. Experiment with direction.

SWAP HEROES
Each character comes with a special ability that can help in battle, so be sure to try out any heroes that you unlock. There are 40 in total!

FAST FACT

Space Invaders dates all the way back to *1978*, while *Arkanoid* followed in *1986*. Both were developed by the legendary Japanese arcade game developer Taito.

ALSO CHECK OUT...

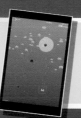

SPACE INVADERS INFINITY GENE
Infinity Gene is another modern riff on the classic arcade blaster, keeping the alien-zapping core while gradually bringing in big bosses and cool new weapons, as well as vibrant colors and pulsing tunes.

BRICKIES
Brickies puts a fun riff on the classic brick-breaking platform game premise as you try to zip through each stage before the timer empties. It also has circular stage designs, unique brick types, and other amusing quirks.

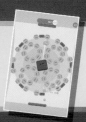

THE CRAZIEST GAMES

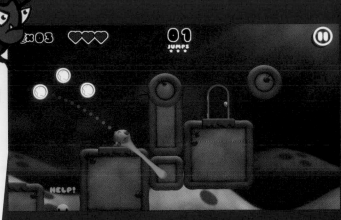

THESE WILL BLOW YOUR MIND

Fed up with playing the same old kind of games? Want to try something a bit different? Then you're in the right place! There are many weird and wonderful ideas for mobile games in the various app stores. Some are new, some are old. Some will make you laugh, others will surprise you. But most are genius in their own, unique way. So where should you start? Let's take a look at the potential cream of the crop . . .

BOOGER BOING

Is this the craziest game ever? Maybe "snot" but it's certainly one of our top picks! It's a gloriously gross jaunt through the inside of a nose and it'll have you using your finger to stretch and flick boogers to complete each level. All you need to do is aim for the green patches, avoid the nasal nasties, and get to the exit in the fewest leaps for the maximum stars.

I AM BREAD

Potentially the best thing since sliced bread, this bizarre game centers on a slice of bread determined to become toast. Help it reach its aim by preventing it from becoming contaminated and tasteless.

GOAT SIMULATOR

You've got to be kidding: a simulator based around a goat? Hey, it's no joke! The game lets you wreak havoc by running, jumping, bashing into things, and licking whatever you want. Plus you have free rein to go anywhere. Feel like taking a goat down a water slide? Yep, this game has you covered.

DOODLE JUMP

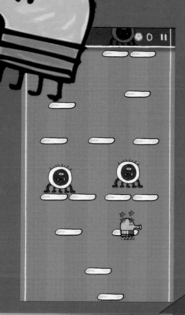

Doodle Jump's graphics look like they've been scribbled on scrap paper, but it's all part of the charm. The wacky game uses your device's accelerometer to control the character as you leap onto platforms and avoid hazards. Cue lots of funny sound effects, too.

SAUSAGE BOMBER

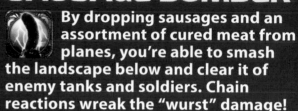

By dropping sausages and an assortment of cured meat from planes, you're able to smash the landscape below and clear it of enemy tanks and soldiers. Chain reactions wreak the "wurst" damage!

ROTATE THE BEAR

Rotate a cute bear as many times as possible to get a high score. But if a bee appears, you must stop or the bear will get stung. But then keep spinning to add more seconds to the clock!

CHICKEN SCREAM

Although created by Perfect Tap Games, you don't actually touch the phone to play! Instead you have to talk or sing to make the chicken walk—or scream to make it jump. The farther your chicken goes, the more points you make.

PINEAPPLE PEN

Created on the back of a bizarre viral music video called *Pen Pineapple Apple Pen*, the concept of this game is simple but crazy with a capital K (for the artist Daimaou Kosaka, of course). Stick a pen into a variety of fruits and aim for the center as closely as possible.

FAST **FACT**

The creators of *Old Man's Journey* were inspired by other emotional titles like *Flower* and *Journey* by thatgamecompany. Highly acclaimed, in 2017, it won Apple's Design Award, among others.

Some of the game's colors are so good you'll just want to sit down and stare at everything. Where's the nearest bench?

OLD MAN'S JOURNEY

A FLOOD OF MEMORIES

Video games are often about death matches and explosive battles, but sometimes you want something a little less intense. *Old Man's Journey* is just that—a gorgeous-looking adventure game where you control an elderly man as he travels through a host of different environments remembering events from his past. Beautiful art and emotional gameplay that may bring a tear to your eye.

TIPS & TRICKS

MOVING MOUNTAINS
Having trouble getting to the next area? Just drag pieces of the landscape around until a completely new path is created.

TAKE A LOAD OFF
Once you get past each puzzle, look for the nearest bench. The old man will sit down and have a dramatic flashback.

WHAT DOES THIS DO?
Each screen in the game is filled with objects to interact with. Move the cursor around and see what you can uncover.

LIKE THIS?
ALSO CHECK OUT...

TENGAMI
Taking place in a Japanese pop-up book, you fold pieces of the paper world to discover new pathways. *Tengami* is colorful and calming, while the music really helps immerse you in the game.

GOROGOA
Drag, drop, slide, and rearrange amazing hand-drawn panels in this unique puzzler. Animations morph, change, and combine in ways that push the surreal story in unexpected new directions.

SCRIBBLENAUTS UNLIMITED

NEXT-LEVEL WORDPLAY

In no other game would a fire-breathing dragon, hot-dog costume, or gargantuan rainbow sword be the solution to any conundrum—but they all work in *Scribblenauts Unlimited*. This one-of-a-kind puzzler tests both your creativity and word knowledge as you tap in terms to drop objects and creatures into the world. Each challenge can be solved in different ways, and it's up to you to think up the zaniest, most useful words possible.

TIPS & TRICKS

EXTRA ADJECTIVES
Go wild on your descriptions of items and characters: adjectives (like "red" or "brave") can impact the way something acts.

TRY AGAIN
Messed up a mission because of an item you summoned? Reset the level from the settings gear icon; you won't lose progress.

CREATE CHAOS
Bored? If you're looking for a destructive twist, summon a meteor, flood, or black hole to shake things up a bit!

FAST FACT

The main character of *Scribblenauts Unlimited* is named Max. He has 41 brothers and one sister who is named Lily. Max was given his magical notebook by his parents, Edgar and Julie.

LIKE THIS? ALSO CHECK OUT...

SCRIBBLENAUTS REMIX
Can't get enough *Scribblenauts* on your smartphone? Loop back to *Remix* when you're done with *Unlimited*. This earlier release is simpler and more straightforward, but still packs in crazy antics.

ADVENTURE TIME GAME WIZARD
Create your own game levels with ease in this inventive game based on the cartoon series. You can build stages in the game or sketch them on paper and scan them in with your phone's camera.

CLASH ROYALE

CLASH OF THE CARD TITANS

Got three minutes? If so, you can experience one of the fiercest and most exciting multiplayer games around in *Clash Royale*. Each quick match pits you against an online rival as you battle to see who has the strongest deck of cards, not to mention the sharpest wits. You'll try to take down the enemy base while protecting your own, and play cards that drop fiery cannonballs, warthog-riding warriors, and other powerful units into the fray. Each match is short but satisfying, and it's hard to resist coming back time and again.

FAST FACT

Clash Royale is a spinoff of earlier mobile strategy smash *Clash of Clans* and features many of the same characters. Somewhat unbelieveably, *Clash of Clans* is now six years old!

TIPS & TRICKS

OPEN THE CHESTS
Winning matches earns treasure chests with free cards and currency. Open them ASAP so that you have room for more.

EXPERIMENT WITH DECKS
Having trouble with your current deck? Swap cards and play with styles to find a well-balanced, rival-dominating combination.

FIND A CLAN
Joining an in-game clan lets you request cards for upgrades and benefit from donating cards to buddies. Swap strategies, too!

ALSO CHECK OUT...

VAINGLORY
Like *Clash Royale*, *Vainglory* is all about destroying enemy towers—but this game is a 5v5 team-based battle for supremacy, and the back-and-forth matches can last 20+ minutes. It's heavy on tactical strategy.

HEARTHSTONE
Like building decks and collecting cards? *Hearthstone* is mobile's top card-battler, challenging you to make the most effective deck possible and then use it to demolish online foes. You'll find no shortage of competition here.

FAST FACT

Dandara is inspired by a Brazilian warrior who fought against slavery during the 17th century. A mysterious figure, she used the martial art capoeira in battle.

DANDARA

TAKING LEAPS OF FAITH

A heroine rises to fight oppression in a directionless world. Unlike other platform adventures, movement is boundless as *Dandara* can jump across floors to walls, ceilings, and many other moving and rotating platforms. The world of Salt is full of secrets and challenges to discover. Unlock new powers, uncover mysteries, survive puzzles and enemies, and prepare for some epic boss fights! With a unique and intuitive control and 360-aiming system, *Dandara* turns the Metroidvania platformer—quite literally—on its head.

TIPS & TRICKS

CHARGE IT UP
You must charge your shots so ensure you have an opening to fire at enemies before landing in a dangerous position.

WHITE LINES
You can only jump onto surfaces that are marked in white. There's also a limit to how far you can jump, shown by an arrow.

GETTING SALTY
Collect salt from defeated enemies and the world. Spend it at campfires for upgrades like increased health.

LIKE THIS? ALSO CHECK OUT…

KERO BLASTER
In this old-school platformer, you play as a frog tasked with defeating monsters who have been infecting teleporters. Run, gun, and jump your way through pixel-art levels.

VVVVVV
Another gravity-defying platformer. Your character can't even jump but instead manipulates gravity to fall up, down, and sideways around a non-linear world, avoiding enemies and traps. For serious gamers.

THE BEST SPORTS GAMES

LIVE OUT YOUR DREAMS

Whether you're into football, baseball, basketball, or practically any sport on the planet, there's a mobile game for everyone. These games allow you to live out your ultimate fantasies, such as scoring the winning goal in the World Cup or making the game-winning touchdown in the Super Bowl. Some of the biggest and most successful mobile games can be found in the world of sports, and we've included the best of the bunch in this list.

FIFA MOBILE

This popular soccer series from EA Sports continues to hit new heights with each passing year—just as it does on PC and consoles. *FIFA Mobile* includes lots of exclusive features, as well as a unique take on the popular "Ultimate Team" mode. The highlight is arguably "VS Attack," which challenges you to play quick, bite-sized games against other online players while scoring as many goals as possible. All the top soccer players are licensed for you to take control of, and by building your squad you can turn any player in the game into a soccer superstar.

ASPHALT 9: LEGENDS

The latest entry in the long-running *Asphalt* series heads back to the track for a racing experience unlike any other. The graphics are truly stunning for a mobile game and there are loads of supercars to collect, which can be raced against the AI and up to eight players online.

WWE SUPERCARD

This collectible card game is one of the best wrestling games of recent years, allowing you to compete in *Top Trumps*-style battles with your squad of WWE superstars. New and exciting cards and gameplay modes are regularly added on for you to try out, so there's always a fun reason to keep playing.

TOUCHGRIND SKATE 2

If you've tried fingerboarding with mini skateboards, you'll know what to expect with this game. It's not easy—it takes time to pull off the best tricks with consistency—but stick with it and you'll be hitting incredible moves such as the "900 Insane Kickflip" in no time.

PAR 4
STROKES 4

SUPER STICKMAN GOLF 3

The third edition of the *Super Stickman Golf* series, first released back in 2016, is the best of the lot. It's very much a typical golf game, but with one key difference: the ball sticks to various objects! That means you can use different obstacles to your advantage, and there are loads of fun course designs that make use of it. The best bit is the multiplayer real-time race mode, which tasks you and your friends with sinking the ball into each hole as quickly as possible. Minigolf at its best!

BOTTOM OF THE 9TH

Bottom of the 9th actually started out as a tabletop game before Handelabra Games got its mitts on it. This is still the same basic game though: it's a fun-filled take on good ol' fashioned baseball. The aim of the game is to hit a home run with the bases loaded in the bottom of the 9th.

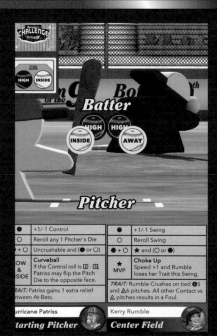

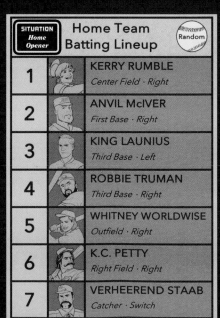

	SITUATION Home Opener	Home Team Batting Lineup	Random
1		KERRY RUMBLE	Center Field · Right
2		ANVIL McIVER	First Base · Right
3		KING LAUNIUS	Third Base · Left
4		ROBBIE TRUMAN	Third Base · Right
5		WHITNEY WORLDWISE	Outfield · Right
6		K.C. PETTY	Right Field · Right
7		VERHEEREND STAAB	Catcher · Switch

NBA 2K18

2K Games has been making incredible basketball games for over a decade, and this one's a great example. On-court gameplay is polished and authentic. The "MyCareer" mode is the highlight, though, allowing you to create your own player and compete in the NBA.

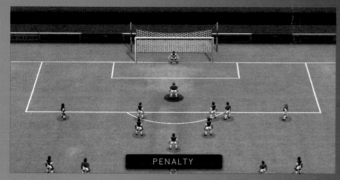

NEW STAR MANAGER

The original *New Star Soccer* was a huge hit, allowing you to control the career of your player both on and off the field. In *NSM*, you manage a whole team! The gameplay makes for a unique soccer simulation.

MADDEN NFL OVERDRIVE

If you're in the mood for some football, it doesn't get any better than this entry in EA Sports' long-running series. Replacing the original *Madden NFL Mobile*, the game boasts fantastic visuals and realistic gameplay, complete with a tactic-enabling Overdrive meter which offers added depth.

VIRTUA TENNIS CHALLENGE

SEGA's popular *Virtua Tennis* series has been going for two decades, but this is the first game on mobile. Gameplay is excellent and the graphics are fantastic. Compete in a huge world tour or against your friends online.

FAST FACT

Animal Crossing: Pocket Camp was downloaded over 15 million times in its first week of release. Despite receiving mixed reviews, it won a raft of gaming industry awards in 2017-2018.

ANIMAL CROSSING: POCKET CAMP

HEADING BACK TO NATURE

The smell of fresh air, the rustling of trees in the background—if you're after an outdoor adventure, *Animal Crossing* has you covered. Build up your own campsite by helping the locals with their chores and you may end up with a new best friend. Your campsite can be whatever you want it to be, and if you want to kick it up a notch, collect resources and you can build your own furniture. In *Animal Crossing: Pocket Camp* you can experience the great outdoors without leaving the house!

TIPS & TRICKS

THE SECRET MONEY TREE
Each day a tree will randomly appear in the world and when you shake it, it drops between 300 and 1,000 bells.

MAKING MONEY
The quickest, and simplest, way to make money in *Animal Crossing* is by catching fish and selling them. So carpe diem: seize the day!

KEEP TALKING
Even when an animal has joined your campsite, it's a good idea to always check in on them every so often and ask how they're doing.

Your camp, your design. Spend time getting to know the locals and they may have some incredible new items for you and your campsite.

LIKE THIS?

ALSO CHECK OUT...

THE TRAIL: FRONTIER CHALLENGE
If you're still yearning for some outdoor fun, *The Trail* takes you on a vast journey through the countryside and features crafting new gear, trading with fellow travelers, and, eventually, building your own settlement.

TRIALS FRONTIER
Okay. If things are a bit peaceful, why not tear up the countryside on the back of a motorcycle in *Trials Frontier*'s often grueling race tracks? It even has its own online multiplayer modes for those looking to throw down with other players.

FAST FACT

Vainglory is without question the best and most popular MOBA available on mobile. You should spend your time and energy here.

There are over 38 heroes in the game. Each of these have different skills and allow for different play styles, but they are all expertly balanced.

VAINGLORY 5V5

STAY IN YOUR LANE

Vainglory is a multiplayer online battle arena (MOBA) that pits two teams of five against one another. Each team grapples for control over three hotly contested lanes. At the end of them is your opponent's main base—destroy it and you can claim victory. Computer-controlled minions can be found moving across the map, fodder to help you level up ahead of fighting other powerful player-controlled enemies. *Vainglory* is easy to play but difficult to master; a game that only gets better the more time you put into it.

TIPS & TRICKS

PRACTICE MAKES PERFECT
Find a character that works for you by taking every hero for a spin in a practice match before playing with others!

STEER CLEAR OF TURRETS
The turrets in the lanes can decimate your health. Stay away from them until you gain a few levels.

DON'T QUIT OUT
Even if you're losing, avoid quitting out. Finishing a game will improve your Karma level, which will ultimately help you unlock new heroes and skins.

LIKE THIS? ALSO CHECK OUT...

HEROES OF ORDER AND CHAOS
One of the first MOBA games to launch on mobile, it has really fun heroes and finely tuned combat. It might be old, but it is still one of the best available.

ARENA OF VALOR
This strategy-focused MOBA lets you choose from over 40 characters in a variety of modes. You can also team up with friends, compete in tournaments, and create leagues.

ROBLOX

Some of *Roblox*'s games can be wacky, but that's part of the fun! Seek out the mad stuff and see just how crazy things can get!

ROBLOX
A MILLION GAMES IN ONE!

What's better than a free game? Why, thousands of free games, of course! *Roblox* is a hub where creative community members post games they've made within *Roblox* for you and your friends to play. The library is vast and no matter what kind of games you like, there'll be something there for you. Racing games, RPGs, competitive multiplayer, adventures, puzzles . . . you name it, you can almost certainly play it in *Roblox*. With so many games to choose from, it can be hard to decide which to play next!

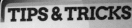

TIPS & TRICKS

FOLLOW THE TRAIL
If you enjoy a game, scroll down to the bottom of its page to find a selection of similar ones to try.

PLAY SAFE
Agree rules with your parents about what kinds of *Roblox* games you can play, and for how long. Using the chat feature? Never give out any personal info.

FOLLOW THE STARS
Seen one of your favorite YouTube stars play something cool or strange in *Roblox*? Search for the game and try it yourself!

LIKE THIS? ALSO CHECK OUT...

GROWTOPIA
A 2-D sandbox adventure that features unique worlds where everything grows on trees, from fruit to jetpacks! While it's not quite as structured as *Roblox*, it does still offer you the chance to play however you want.

MINETEST

You probably guessed from the title and the picture, but this one is a bit like *Minecraft*! It's got that style, but its many game types makes it feel more like *Roblox*; it's a blend of both.

TOP 5...GAMES

DINOSAUR SIMULATOR

2 Survival games are common in *Roblox*, but this one is fun as it does away with standard characters. Instead, pick one of the featured dinosaurs and roam the prehistoric land in search of food and friends. Help your species evolve, but watch out for predators!

EGG FARM SIMULATOR

3 This plays like many online 'clicker'-type games—harvest eggs to hire more helpers, who will in turn help you tame more powerful chickens and score even more eggs! There's loads to unlock and the more you play, the more familiar faces will join your egg-collecting army!

NATURAL DISASTER SURVIVAL

1 An older *Roblox* game, but it's fun so still attracts many players. You're dropped into an arena for an impending disaster—some are silly, others are serious. Simply work together with the other players to find a way to stay alive until the next round!

FAST FACT
Roblox (meaning robots and blocks) isn't as new as you might think: work first started on it in 2004, when it was still called *DynaBlocks*! It now has over 70 million monthly active players.

FREEZE TAG

4 Even the simplest game concepts can be a lot of fun in *Roblox*, as this old classic proves. Players are divided into runners and chasers, the escaping team sprinting and leaping around cool maps to try and avoid the ice-cold touch of their pursuers. Can you avoid meeting a chilly end?

ROYALE HIGH

5 Put on your fanciest outfit and get ready for school life in a fantasy world! Epic castles, flowing gowns, and magical adventures are standard. Even things like going to classes are fun in this cool fairytale setting. *Roblox* has a ton of school games, but none as classy as this!

This is an unofficial/unauthorized guide to *Roblox*

SHOWCASE

POLY BRIDGE

Poly Bridge asks you to put on your engineering hat as you build bridges to solve physics-based puzzles. Each vehicle type has its own weight and speed that you must think about when building. The trial-and-error gameplay keeps you thinking and makes you want to replay levels to experiment with new designs.

Every world has a custom color palette to give it personality. The general look is still consistent throughout the game.

The designers didn't want the game to look realistic so they chose a fun design that wouldn't take away from the bridge-building.

The concept art, level assets, and promotional material were all created using the same program.

Halfway through development, the look of the game was completely changed. Here is an early screenshot.

The vehicles in *Poly Bridge* were all based on existing designs, but tweaked to fit the style of the game.

THE BEST INDIE GAMES

SEARCHING FOR INDIE INSPIRATION

One of the great things about mobile is how easy it is for small teams of indie creators to get their games out there. It makes mobile a great place to find games full of fresh and creative ideas. In fact, indie developers have shown that they can compete with the biggest companies in the world by making some of the best titles on mobile. Here is a list of games that proves it.

ATOMIK: RUNGUNJUMPGUN

There are only two buttons in this game: one makes you shoot forward and one makes you shoot down, propelling your character up in the air. Using these two buttons you whizz through intense 2-D platforming levels that will push your skills to the limit.

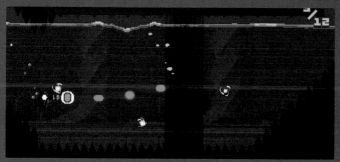

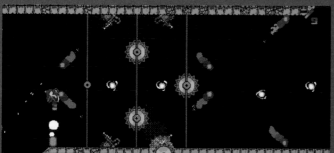

KENSHŌ

In *Kenshō*, you must slide blocks to match them up and solve puzzles to advance the game's story. Thanks to *Kenshō*'s beautiful art and calming music, the game's world is a lovely place to spend some time doing some relaxing puzzling.

RADIUM 2

You have to navigate a ball through over 130 tricky stages, featuring tight tunnels and dangerous saws, using two tractor beams in this cool, slickly-made, fast-moving, physics-based puzzle.

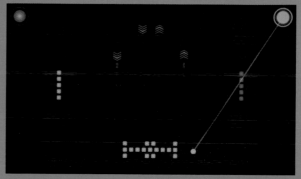

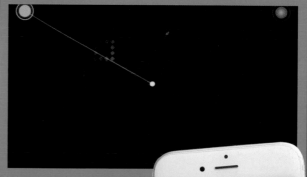

FLAT PACK

The levels in this game are 3-D, but your character is 2-D. It sounds confusing, but once you start exploring how your character can wrap around the corners, you'll get it. We love the clever perspective twists and boss fights!

SILLY WALKS

Silly Walks is one of those games you can play casually with one hand. Your character spins on one foot until you tap to step, at which point it switches to the other foot. Use these controls to navigate through levels and complete objectives. It's lots of fun and very goofy.

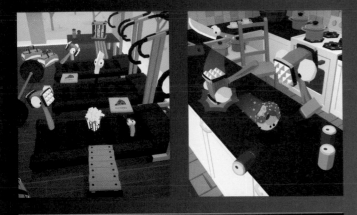

THE OFFICE QUEST

It's just another boring day in the office, until your character decides he's had enough and wants to find a way out. *The Office Quest* is a mix of comedy and point-and-click adventure where you'll meet funny characters and solve tricky puzzles on your way to escaping the office!

F AST FACT

The shapes that you play with in the minimalist puzzler *Unbalance* are partly inspired by Islamic geometry. Produced by Turkish developer Tvee it's the ideal game for fans of physics.

YELLOW

The goal in this game is simple: turn your entire screen yellow. But what makes things interesting is that this objective alters on every level; there is always a different way to turn your device yellow. That means you have to experiment and discover the tricks to solve each specific puzzle. You might need to erase something, tap a button, or slide shapes. Successfully detecting the solution is the fun part.

UNBALANCE

You start each level in *Unbalance* with a simple shape containing balls inside. Twist the shape and the balls will start to roll around along the lines as gravity does its work. The idea is to twist the shape so that the red ball falls into a target at the bottom of the screen.

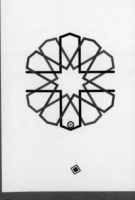

THE BIG JOURNEY

 In *The Big Journey* you take control of a cute, chubby little kitty named Mr. Whiskers. By turning the screen, you help Mr. Whiskers roll around the world on his journey to find a missing dumpling.

.PROJEKT

If you like the cool perspective puzzling of the *Monument Valley* games, then you should give this one a try. Your goal is to build up a 3-D shape that will cast shadows that match two different 2-D shapes drawn on two walls.

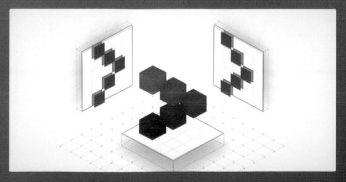

WARLOCK'S TOWER

With every step you take in *Warlock's Tower*, you lose one life. That means you must carefully plan your path through each level to collect extra lives on the way and get safely to the exit. There are over 100 tricky levels for you to play through.

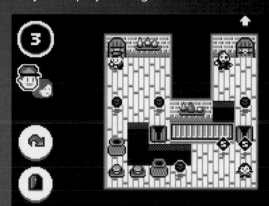

FERN FLOWER

 In *Fern Flower*, you jump up a mountain trying to climb as high as you can. You can collect fireflies to boost your score and fern flowers to unlock new characters and power-ups.

KAMI 2

Each puzzle in *Kami 2* is a beautiful design. Your goal is to flood that design with one color in as few moves as possible. As well as having over 100 puzzles for you to play, the game has a build mode that lets you create your own for others to enjoy.

FAST FACT

The puzzles in *Kami 2* are made by hand, cut from real paper using scalpels, and then photographed. You can make your own design using the "Puzzle Builder" and challenge others to beat your score.

CAPTAIN TOM GALACTIC TRAVELER

You get to explore whole galaxies, flying from planet to planet and running around to grow flowers in this fun mobile platformer. Captain Tom will stay stuck to planets without falling off, until you're ready to use your jetpack to boost off and find another one!

A PLANET OF MINE

In this game you develop your own civilization by exploring new planets, gathering resources, discovering new species, placing buildings, and trading or fighting with the other factions you will meet as your civilization grows. It's a great mix of resource management, strategy, and exploration.

I LOVE HUE

I Love Hue is a simple and relaxing puzzle game about playing with color. Each puzzle presents you with a grid of colors that gradually shifts between shades. The catch is that some colors will be in the wrong place, so it's your job to put them in the correct slot.

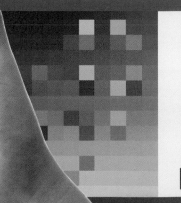

SINKR

On each stage of this game you will see a series of holes and pucks. Your goal is to use the contraptions in the stage to get all the pucks into the holes. It starts off simple, but each level gets more difficult as new ideas are added to challenge your puzzling skills.

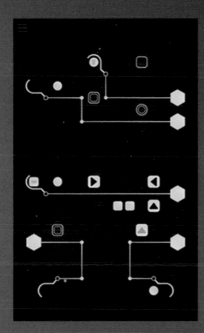

OLD MAN'S JOURNEY

This has to be one of the most stunning-looking games you can play on mobile. You take control of an old man who travels through villages, towns, countryside, and across the sea on trains, boats, and balloons. You interact with the beautiful environments to solve simple puzzles and help him on his way.

DESERT GOLFING

Desert Golfing is exactly what it sounds like: a game where you play golf in the desert. Each time you complete a hole, the game generates a new one, so you never run out of tricky golfing challenges to complete.

FAST FACT

While *Desert Golfing* has no ending due to its continually generating stages, in early builds of the game some of the later levels were impossible, creating an unintentional ending.

ALTO'S ODYSSEY

Alto's Odyssey puts you in control of a snowboarder gliding through a beautiful landscape. You can chain combos together by pulling off huge leaps, cool tricks, riding on walls, grinding on vines, and bouncing off balloons to send you soaring into the sky. Unlock new characters as you play and get power-ups, like a wing suit that you can use to glide through the sky. You'll last longer every time you play!

Not in the mood for adventure? Turn your hand to crafting instead and see what kind of amazing buildings and settlements you can create!

FAST FACT

Terraria is one of the most successful recent indie games, having sold over 20 million copies across all platforms since its release in 2011.

TERRARIA
YOUR WORLD, YOUR WAY!

If you love *Minecraft*, you'll probably love *Terraria*, too! With the game being 2-D rather than 3-D, it's even easier to make epic creations. Adventuring is simpler, too, but don't assume that makes *Terraria* an easy game. Far from it, in fact. While you can just build a fancy home and defend it, the real challenge comes when you get out to slay the bosses in the wilderness. If you want—but there's nothing to stop you having fun just building.

TIPS & TRICKS

HOME SWEET HOME
It's a good idea to build a base near useful resources, so try to make your home between two different biomes if possible.

BIGGER IS BETTER
The small sprites can make *Terraria* tricky to play well on a phone. Play on a tablet if possible, it's much easier to see.

GEAR UP!
Don't spend all your materials on building. Be sure to craft new equipment before anything else, as it will help you progress faster.

LIKE THIS? ALSO CHECK OUT...

MINECRAFT
This one should need no introduction! *Terraria* is basically a 2-D version of *Minecraft*, so go see Steve and pals if you want to be even more immersed in your own sandbox survival world!

JUNK JACK
Slightly more laid back than *Terraria*, but just as enjoyable if you're in the mood for something a little more chilled out. It's all very familiar, so it's perfect for when you've done all you can in *Terraria*.

ALPHABEAR 2

ALMOST UN-BEAR-ABLY CHARMING

What's even more delightful than the bear-centric world-building game, *Alphabear*? *Alphabear 2*, of course, which keeps the same alluring premise while introducing even sillier bears, not to mention a wacky time-travel story around the wordplay. Luckily, the core concept is still fantastic: you'll spell out words using the visible *Scrabble*-like letter tiles, which expire after a certain number of rounds. Can you clear them all and fill the screen with a giant bear instead? That's the hilarious, brain-teasing task ahead of you.

TIPS & TRICKS

USE THE BEARS
Each bear you bring into a stage comes with special abilities and bonuses, so know your bears' benefits before building.

WATCH THE TILES
See that number on each tile? When it hits zero, the tile turns to stone and it's useless. Always use letters before they're wasted.

BUILD A BEAR
Growing the bears is key to maxing out your score. Try to use tiles nearest to the bears to boost their size and fill the board!

NEW BEAR!

Alphabear 2 has loads of individually stylized bears, each of which brings a unique score boost and ability when you equip it for a level.

...zzle Bear
...R PARTY!
...t +1 Tile

First, I'm going to hit a clock tower with a lightning bolt, and—

FAST FACT

Alphabear isn't even developer Spry Fox's first bear-themed game—that'd be adorable mobile matching puzzler, *Triple Town*.

LIKE THIS? ALSO CHECK OUT...

FOUR LETTERS
Four Letters is another word-building game, but this one is all about speed: you'll have just seconds to build a four-letter word and then repeat as many times as possible. It's surprisingly thrilling!

LETTERPRESS
Letterpress puts a competitive spin on word games: facing an online foe, you'll take turns building terms to try and conquer more and more of the letter grid. Will your color prevail in the end?

⏸ 1 more

🕐 039

Helping the farmer load his produce onto his wagon is a simple job to ease you into the mechanics before things get wackier.

PART TIME UFO

JOBS ON THE FLY

Remember those claw machines you try to win toys from in arcades and amusement parks? How about playing as one from outer space, who's come to Earth to help humans out with their problems?

As a UFO, you'll fly around over 25 stages, and be given a range of inventive and bizarre jobs. From helping a clumsy museum assistant put an exhibit back together to stacking cheerleaders to form a pyramid, there are plenty of ways to make money. A cute, charming, and challenging game unlike anything else.

FAST FACT

Part Time UFO is made by HAL Laboratory, best known for creating *Kirby* for Nintendo consoles. This is their first ever mobile game but it has received top reviews.

TIPS & TRICKS

DRESS UP
Use money you earn from jobs to buy new outfits. Not only do they look cool, each outfit also helpfully changes the mechanics.

PRO BONUS
Each job has three objectives, but only icons provide hints on what you have to do. Complete all three objectives to get paid more!

ONE-HANDED PLAY
There are separate touchscreen buttons for movement and crane, but you can also change settings to play with just one hand.

SUPER MARIO RUN
In a way, *Part Time UFO* is a quirky platformer. But if you're after something a bit more traditional, there's nothing better than Nintendo's own *Super Mario*! Simple to play with tap controls and full of fun challenges.

TINY BUBBLES
There are a fair amount of physics-based puzzles in *Part Time UFO* but you might prefer something a little bit more laid back. Blow, combine, and pop bubbles of the same color, and get some help from a little fish friend, too.

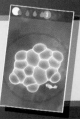

OCMO

SWING YOUR WAY TO VICTORY

Ocmo is a very tough physics-based platformer but you'll soon get into the swing of things. After all, reaching the end of each of the 80 levels requires more than walking or jumping—you can grab a piece of scenery with one of the creature's tentacles and swing between the surfaces. The aim is to figure out the best moment to tap or press the screen. Get it wrong, and the creature will splat against an object forcing you to try again. The reward for a win is a tasty bunny!

TIPS & TRICKS

USE LONG TENTACLES
Don't get too close to an object you want to grab. Better to have a longer tentacle to give more time for your next move.

TRY A SPEEDRUN
Ocmo feels great when you try to play it as fast as you can. This lets you create longer swings and helps retain a chosen direction.

KEEP TRYING
Everybody makes a mistake in *Ocmo*, which is why it has unlimited lives. The more you play, the better you'll become.

FAST **FACT**

It took five years for the developer to complete the game because of the detailed physics calculations required for the main character's moves.

The levels become harder as you progress, but complete them really quickly and you will unlock even tougher Dark World versions.

LIKE THIS? ALSO CHECK OUT…

TENTACLES – ENTER THE MIND
Just like *Ocmo*, you control a tentacled creature making its way around its world by clinging on to one object after another. Tap the screen to travel over the courses.

HANGER – ROPE SWING
The stickman in this game is like Spider-Man but without the special powers. He uses a rope to swing around and you must stop him dropping to the floor. Unlock characters along the way.

These contraptions look simple to begin with. Of course, you need to figure out how to open them up to reveal the wonders within.

FAST FACT

GNOG also includes optional augmented reality support for iOS devices, adding a whole other level of tactile physical interaction.

GNOG
A TOY BOX OF TRICKS

A delightful experience to tinker with your curiosity, *GNOG* is a series of elaborate toy boxes made up of large monster heads, waiting to be opened up. Inside these wondrous creations are intricate interactive puzzles you can press, pull, slide, grab, click, and rotate. With nine uniquely tactile monster heads to explore, it's one of the most colorful and vibrant experiences on mobile. A dynamic soundtrack complements the puzzles, building and building as you discover another magical moment.

TIPS & TRICKS

SIGHT AND SOUND
Interactivity is emphasized by changes in visuals and sound to guide you what to do next. Headphones are recommended.

TOUCH EVERYTHING
It's not always clear what you can interact with, so just try touching everything to begin with!

SEARCHING FOR SECRETS
As a game about being playfully curious, not everything you do actually leads to solving the puzzle, but you may still get something neat happening.

LIKE THIS?
ALSO CHECK OUT...

 VIGNETTES
This is also an interactive exploration game without text or characters. Filled with seemingly normal objects, spin them around and discover kaleidoscopic puzzles. Accessible to everyone.

 PRUNE
With a minimalist style inspired by Japanese art, this is a much simpler but no less remarkable puzzle game. Like bonsai, it's all about pruning trees. A very peaceful experience that will grow on you.

LINELIGHT
THE LIGHT FANTASTIC

In this puzzle game you control a sliver of white light that travels along thin pathways suspended in space. The aim is simply to continue onward, but doing so requires getting past enemies, doors, and moving platforms. It looks very simple, but *Linelight* can be incredibly tricky. The game never punishes you, though—there's no time limit and you get infinite lives. It's all about you, the puzzles, and the funky beat playing in the background as you work on your next solution.

FAST FACT

Each color of light has a unique behavior. Understanding how the lights move is the key to solving puzzles. The red, orange, pink, and purple lights may move independently or with you.

TIPS & TRICKS

EXPERIMENT
Linelight has many checkpoints. Try new approaches to puzzles; loss only means a minor setback.

KEEP YOUR COOL
This game is one of logic and rhythm. If you fail at a puzzle, look at how the enemies behave, and adjust your timing.

FIND THE STARS
Check out the world map and you'll see little dots floating in space. Find the hidden pathways to them and you'll be rewarded with a green star.

LIKE THIS? ALSO CHECK OUT...

OUTFOLDED
Like *Linelight*, this game requires you to discover pathways to travel through an abstract world. Only this time, you control a solid shape and one of its sides vanishes after every move—until there are none left.

FROST
Like *Linelight*, *Frost* is another stunning-looking puzzle game that revolves around light. Your job is to guide little spirits through space, creating incredible light shows as you progress.

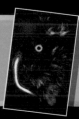

THE BEST VR GAMES

GET IMMERSED IN THESE GAMES

You don't need a powerful PC, console, or a pricey headset to try virtual reality—today's smartphones can also enable incredible VR experiences. The Samsung Gear VR and Google Daydream headsets let you snap in a compatible phone and then immerse yourself in game worlds that surround you from all angles. Google Cardboard is another mobile VR option, and it works with both Android phones and iPhones. Eager to try VR's best games? Start with these inventive gems . . .

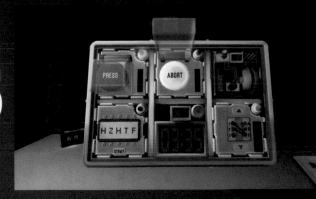

KEEP TALKING AND NOBODY EXPLODES

Here's a rare multiplayer virtual reality game: one player wears the headset while looking at a ticking time bomb, while the other players shout commands from a printable "bomb defusal manual" outside of the game. Can you work together to disarm the bomb, or will you trigger an explosive finale?

PROTON PULSE

Proton Pulse **puts a VR spin on classic brick-breaking games, as you control the paddle with head movements to hit the ball back into the arena. It's straightforward, but incredibly fun.**

MINECRAFT

Maybe you've played *Minecraft* on a smartphone or tablet, TV, or computer screen. But you haven't really lived in a *Minecraft* world until you've strapped it onto your face! That's what the "Gear VR" version lets you do, as you explore the blocky worlds and create fun things or survive vicious threats. The game takes on a whole new feel when you can look around.

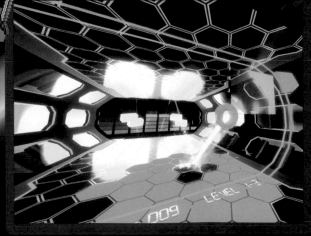

LAND'S END

The best mobile VR games keep things simple, and that's true with *Land's End*, an enchanting adventure from the makers of *Monument Valley*. Here, you'll explore natural terrain and solve a series of mysterious puzzles that lack complexity, but keep you curious. It's big on atmosphere and thankfully free of frustration.

CAAAAARDBOARD!

One of Google Cardboard's best games is simply titled *Caaaaardboard!*, which is what you might yell as your character leaps off buildings and performs stunts. It's a wild one!

REZ INFINITE

Rez Infinite is an incredibly immersive VR experience. As a neon avatar trying to protect a computer network, you'll blast viral code and battle tricky bosses. Dazzling wireframe graphics and banging techno music.

SMASH HIT

Smash Hit began life as a mobile touchscreen game, but it's truly amazing in virtual reality. Lob shiny metal balls to break glass sculptures and panes, which you'll encounter at a rapid pace as you're whisked through tight corridors. Surreal, frenzied, and endless stuff to smash.

ROMANS FROM MARS

This fun tower-defense game is even better in 360-degree VR. You are the last line of defense and must protect your castle from waves of alien invaders using arrows and magic spells. Upgrade your equipment to take on ever more powerful foes.

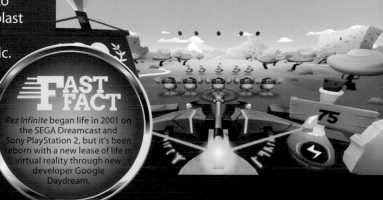

FAST FACT

Rez Infinite began life in 2001 on the SEGA Dreamcast and Sony PlayStation 2, but it's been reborn with a new lease of life in virtual reality through new developer Google Daydream.

THE BEST AR GAMES

GAMING IN THE REAL WORLD

Augmented reality games take the characters and levels you usually see on your smartphone and put them in the world around you. Well, kind of: these AR experiences actually use your phone's camera to transpose the game into your surroundings. That's how you can see Pokémon traipsing around your neighborhood, or game levels set atop your coffee table. And unlike virtual reality, you don't need a headset to experience AR games. Grab these fun picks and give it a shot!

ARISE

Arise drops 3-D game levels right into the world around you and challenges you to guide a small knight to the goal in each. You won't tap or swipe in this game—it's all about looking around the floating stage and finding the right angle to help the hero traverse obstacles.

POKÉMON GO

Pokémon GO is the mobile sensation that hooked more than 800 million players worldwide. It turns Nintendo's beloved series into an augmented reality experience, based on your real surroundings and populated with digital creatures, PokéStops, and Gyms. Grab your Poké Balls and go!

FAST FACT

Pokémon: Let's Go, Pikachu! and *Pokémon: Let's Go, Eevee!*— two games from Nintendo— let you transfer characters from *Pokémon GO*.

⊙ Squirtle   CP 321

Walk with your buddy!

0.4/**1** KM

13.4 km total walked!

GNOG

This imaginative delight provides a series of vibrant and surprising toy-like puzzle boxes to tinker and fiddle with, and *GNOG*'s AR mode brings those dreamlike objects into your environment.

STACK AR

Stack AR turns the act of building block towers into a tricky AR challenge. Each new block hovers over the stack, and if you don't place it perfectly, the top surface is trimmed down—that makes it harder to place the next one. Keep going until you run out of space!

INGRESS

This *Pokémon GO* predecessor similarly turns your real world into a game map, but swaps the cute creatures for futuristic energy sources that you'll try to control with your chosen team.

EUCLIDEAN LANDS

This brainy puzzler takes on a whole new dimension thanks to its AR mode. You'll rotate each Rubik's Cube-like stage to help a small warrior get the jump on his foes and reach the goal. Now you can see the levels from any angle as they float in your space.

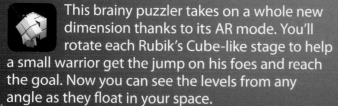

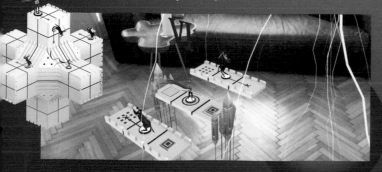

SPLITTER CRITTERS

Splitter Critters was already one of the most inventive mobile games in recent memory, and now it's one of the most enticing AR experiences as well. As before, the goal in *Splitter Critters* is to swipe the screen to tear up the game world, and then move part of that world to create brand new paths for your little alien creatures to traverse. Rather than augment the existing levels, a new AR mode features brand new challenges that you'll play on a box that appears in front of you.

SMASH TANKS

Tanks usually shoot things, right? Well, in *Smash Tanks*, their main mode of attack is slamming into things instead—and you're the one doing the flinging. Each battlefield appears right in front of you via the AR tech, and you'll launch the tanks to smash targets, buildings, and rival tanks.

HEARTHSTONE
THE CARD GAME OF HEROES!

Card games can be super fun, but they can also be very complicated. The beauty of *Hearthstone* is that it's incredibly easy to pick up, with clear card powers and abilities that make it easy to make great moves and also read those of your opponents. There are so many possible decks that you're bound to be able to create one you love, and there are tons of powerful Legendary cards to collect, which can make your deck even stronger! Choose your hero, build your deck, and crush your enemies!

TIPS & TRICKS

HIGHS AND LOWS
Build your deck with a selection of cards of all values. Cheap cards help in the early game, but you'll want some powerful ones for the later stages!

DUST TO DUST
Cards you don't want or need can be dismantled for Dust. Use this to craft cards that will actually be helpful in your favorite deck.

MASTER THE ARENA
Short on great cards? Arena runs let you build temporary draft decks using random cards and the rewards can be great—give it a try!

FAST FACT
Hearthstone (originally named *Hearthstone: Heroes of Warcraft*) now has over 1,500 different cards to collect, which is one of the highest out of all the collectible card games (CCG) on mobile.

Even when things seem bleak, there's always the chance for a crazy comeback. Never lose hope, and try to play your cards right!

LIKE THIS? ALSO CHECK OUT…

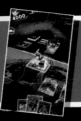

YU-GI-OH! DUEL LINKS
Duel Links streamlines the usual *Yu-Gi-Oh* dueling to use fewer cards, making it great for both beginners and experienced players who want much quicker games. New card collections are added all the time, too!

ASCENSION
If you like the card deck-building fun of *Hearthstone's* Arena, games like *Ascension* offer an even more involved version of CCG (collectible card game) gameplay. You build a new deck every time you play, and they will always be different!

OCEANHORN 2: KNIGHTS OF THE LOST REALM

ADVENTURE IS OUT THERE!

Oceanhorn 2 has the same magic as the original, only now everything is bigger, better, and more awesome! Travel through sprawling maps using new third-person gameplay, outrun tumbling boulders, crawl through ancient ruins, and destroy dangerous enemies with a fresh combat system. There's even a grappling hook to launch and cool new vehicles to ride. This is one epic adventure!

TIPS & TRICKS

VROOM!
Tired of traveling by foot? Why not hop on a vehicle and zip around the game's large maps at top speed. Sure beats walking!

CITY LIFE
Capital, a bustling central town, is a big part of Oceanhorn 2. From here you can start countless different adventures.

HOOK, LINE, & SINKER
If you see a hard-to-reach area, try highlighting it with the cursor and using your grappling hook to launch yourself into the air. Up, up, and away!

Feeling a bit overwhelmed by all the quests in Oceanhorn 2? Find some water and take a quick swim to cool off. Geronimo!

FAST FACT
Oceanhorn 2 is a huge game, but just a handful of people helped to create it—only six developers were on the team!

LIKE THIS? ALSO CHECK OUT...

ADVENTURES OF MANA
This amazing RPG is actually a remake of a Game Boy game from way back in 1991. There's still the same interesting story and tons of fast-paced combat, only now the graphics are way better.

BEAST QUEST!
Slay growling monsters and explore the massive open world of Avantia in this fantasy RPG based on the popular Beast Quest books. You can also hunt down treasure and conquer difficult challenges. Are you brave enough?

THE BEST RETRO GAMES

BUILDING A CLASSIC COLLECTION

It's always exciting to play new games, but we shouldn't forget that gaming history is full of classic games that are still lots of fun to play. Thanks to the power of modern mobile devices, we can play these classics—for which you once needed a console and TV to play—in the palm of our hand and enjoy them on the go. We've picked out some of the best retro games you can play on mobile, including iconic arcade games, strategic RPGs, and exciting action games.

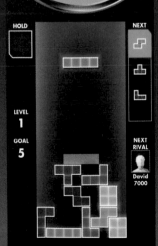

FAST FACT

Tetris is estimated to have sold almost 500 million copies since its original release in 1984. It was designed and programmed by Russian computer engineer Alexey Pajitnov.

TETRIS

It's one of the best-selling games of all time and through mobiles, it's as easy to play as ever. A series of shapes fall from the top of the screen to the bottom. You must turn, move, and slot them into place to match up colors and make the matching blocks disappear for points. This version adds some new modes for you to play, along with the traditional marathon mode.

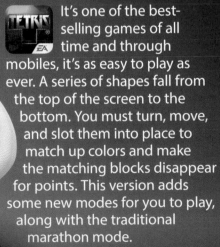

HOLD

NEXT

LEVEL
1

GOAL
5

NEXT
RIVAL

David
7000

DOUBLE DRAGON TRILOGY

What's better than a cool retro game? Three retro games in one. This package contains the first three games in the side-scrolling beat-'em-up series *Double Dragon* where you must fight your way through mean streets, either alone, or with a friend via Bluetooth.

Q*BERT REBOOTED

You can play this mobile version of *Q*bert* in its original 2-D form or in the updated 3-D form. You must hop between cubes to change their color while running from Coily, Ugg, Slick, Sam, Wrong-Way, and Red Ball who will be trying to catch you.

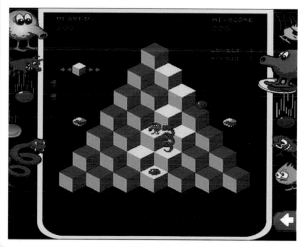

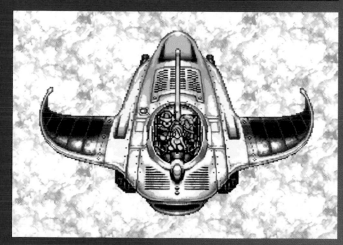

CHRONO TRIGGER

You travel across time and space to meet and recruit a colorful cast of characters to help you save the world in *Chrono Trigger*. Each character has their own backstory and different strengths and skills to help you win turn-based battles against the many monsters, robots, and other enemies you'll face.

NETHACK

Originally released all the way back in a far-off time known as 1987, *NetHack* is a game where you explore randomly generated dungeons filled with armor, spellbooks, potions, and other useful items that you can use to help you defeat enemies—although you never really know what an item will do until you try it!

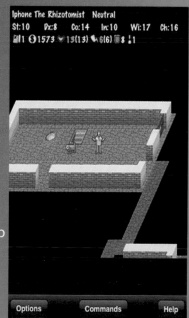

CRAZY TAXI CLASSIC

Pick up a fare and drive to your destination as quickly as possible, making huge jumps, weaving through traffic, and skidding around corners to rack up as many points as you can. *Crazy Taxi* is still a thrilling and fun take on racing that's unlike anything else out there.

BREAKOUT: BOOST

This updated version of an arcade classic is still as much fun as it always was. You have to juggle a ball bouncing on the screen using your paddle, directing it toward the bricks to knock them out. Some cool power-ups and different kinds of bricks add some nice twists to the game.

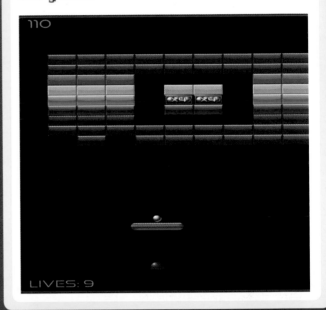

GUNSTAR HEROES CLASSIC

Gunstar Heroes is known as one of the greatest games on SEGA's Genesis. In this exciting run-and-gun game, you can collect a variety of cool weapons, including missiles and lasers, that you can mix in 14 different combinations. There are a host of different enemies to take out, epic boss battles, and you can even play with a friend via WiFi.

ATARI'S GREATEST HITS

You get the classic *Missile Command* game for free with this package and can choose to pay to add 100 other Atari classics to your collection, including the likes of *Asteroids, Centipede,* and *Tempest.*

SECRET OF MANA

This influential game has a reputation as one of the best among fans of JRPGs. In *Secret of Mana* you go on an epic adventure to discover the secrets of a mystical power called Mana and stop an evil empire from taking over the world.

METAL SLUG X

This remake of *Metal Slug 2* adds some new elements to the game, even going so far as to remix all its levels so that you meet enemies and bosses at different points compared to the original. However, the thrilling and chaotic run-and-gun action that made the *Metal Slug* series legendary remains the same.

DECAP ATTACK CLASSIC

 Playing as a surreal-looking monster wrapped in bandages, you have a detachable head that you can throw at enemies in your quest to save the world in this reborn SEGA platformer.

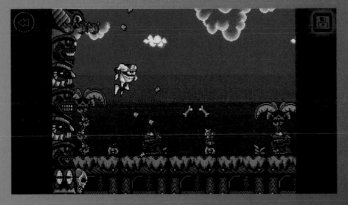

FINAL FANTASY IV

 When the debate about ranking the best games in the legendary *Final Fantasy* series comes up, *Final Fantasy IV* is always one of the contenders thanks to its clever battle system and great story. It is one of the most epic adventures you can experience on mobile.

FINAL FANTASY TACTICS: THE WAR OF THE LIONS

 The depth and level of strategy in this turn-based tactics game can make it tricky to get into, but it's worth it. With an exciting story, interesting characters, and a menu-based battle system perfect for mobile controls, it comes highly recommended for expert gamers.

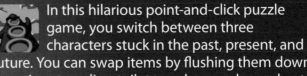

DAY OF THE TENTACLE REMASTERED

In this hilarious point-and-click puzzle game, you switch between three characters stuck in the past, present, and future. You can swap items by flushing them down your time-traveling toilet to solve puzzles and get closer to your ultimate goal of stopping the evil purple tentacle from taking over the world.

SONIC THE HEDGEHOG 2 CLASSIC

This faithful re-creation of SEGA's famous mascot's most well-known game sees you speeding through levels, collecting rings and using your spin attack on robots along the way to defeating the evil Dr. Eggman. This mobile version of everyone's fave hedgehog includes a new zone called "The Hidden Palace Zone" that was taken out of the original release.

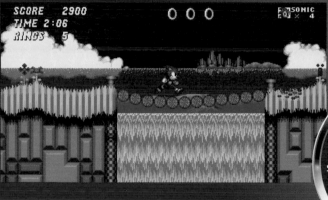

PAC-MAN

It's one of the most famous video games of all time and it's still lots of fun to play all these years later. Guide your Pac-Man around a huge collection of mazes, avoiding the ghosts as you try to chomp all the dots in a level to complete it and move onto the next one. Simple!

FAST FACT

Before SEGA settled on the name Sonic the Hedgehog for the titular protagonist when his first game was released in 1991, one of the early ideas for his name was Mr. Needlemouse!

ROLLERCOASTER TYCOON CLASSIC

A mix of features from *RollerCoaster Tycoon* and *RollerCoaster Tycoon 2*, this management game is all about building the best amusement park you can. By creating thrilling rollercoasters for customers to ride, you can attract more people to your park and use their money to make it even better.

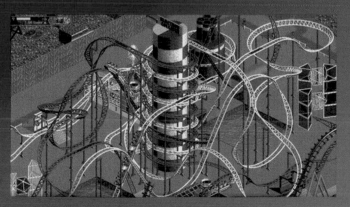

R-TYPE

Dealing with all the enemy ships swarming the screen in this classic arcade blaster is no easy task, but taking the time to master the game so that you can blow away waves of baddies and huge bosses, using awesome weapons and power-ups, is a lot of fun.

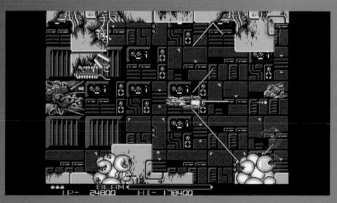

FAST FACT

Ubisoft's *Just Dance* series turns ten years old in 2019. The original game was actually a Nintendo Wii exclusive and it was titled after the Lady Gaga song of the same name.

There's no limit to the number of players that can play in multiplayer sessions. If everyone has a compatible smartphone, they're good to go!

JUST DANCE NOW

DON'T STOP MOVIN'

Don't have a console to play *Just Dance*? Doesn't matter. All you need to play *Just Dance Now* is a phone and a compatible screen—whether that's a smart TV, laptop, or even a tablet. There's a huge library of songs to choose from, hand-picked from the series' massive back catalog of famous hits, and there are loads of routines to go with it. Your phone acts as the controller and it's up to you to match the moves of the dancer on the screen.

TIPS & TRICKS

DON'T FORGET TO STRETCH
If you're going to be doing exercise, preparation is key. Be sure to stretch ahead of time to avoid injury.

THE BIGGER THE BETTER
Just Dance Now can be played on a whole range of screens, but complicated routines are easiest to follow on a TV or large monitor.

STAY ONE STEP AHEAD
You can always see which dance moves are coming next by following the prompts in the bottom right-hand corner of the screen.

LIKE THIS? ALSO CHECK OUT...

BOUNDEN
Grab a friend, hold each side of the phone, and maneuver a crosshair around the sphere on the screen. Before you know it, you'll both be dancing ballet. Crazy, huh?!

PIANO TILES 2
Keep the music flowing by tapping the correct piano keys in order. It's a simple concept, but makes for a game that's tough to put down once you've started.

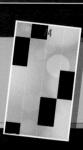

POKÉMON GO

STILL GOTTA CATCH 'EM ALL!

It was one of the biggest app launches ever, but even over two years later, *Pokémon GO* is still one of the most-played mobile games. Developer Niantic has been extremely active in updating the game frequently, with hundreds of new monsters to find and catch in the real world, and new events that bring players together like never before. Trainers can now trade Pokémon, send gifts to friends, and engage in epic multiplayer battles against powerful Raid bosses. Do you have what it takes to be the very best, like no one ever was? Get out there and prove it!

TIPS & TRICKS

SPIN TO WIN
Curveballs give a better chance of capture than regular throws, so learn to hit small targets with spinning balls for more catches!

FRIENDS FOREVER!
Add friends to your in-game list. Exchange a certain number of gifts and you'll get bonuses like extra damage and balls.

STAYING SAFE
Be safe when playing *Pokémon GO*. Don't go out alone, be aware of your surroundings, and never go anywhere you shouldn't.

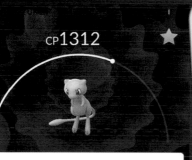

CP1312

Mew
110 / 110 HP

3.45kg	PSYCHIC	0.36m
		HEIGHT

CP663

Growlithe
HP 68 / 68

Fire Type	13.02 kg Weight	0.61 m Height

60606 STARDUST

52 GROWLITHE CANDY

POWER UP — 2200 — 2

EVOLVE — 50

FAST FACT

Pokémon GO is one of the biggest mobile games of all time, with well over 800 million downloads to date across all devices. It has been credited with promoting physical exercise!

35
LukemonPlay

LIKE THIS? ALSO CHECK OUT...

INGRESS
Created by the same team that brought us *Pokémon GO*, in *Ingress* you must team up with other players as you move through the real world to discover and tap on sources of a mysterious energy.

POKÉMON QUEST
Want more Pokémon on your mobile? There are a few options out there, but this cute and chunky adventure is among the better ones. Don't forget to play the wonderfully silly *Magikarp Jump*, too!

SHOWCASE

MONUMENT VALLEY 2

The first *Monument Valley* has been downloaded over 30 million times and won numerous awards. The sequel had to stand out. It did this by introducing two new main characters, a more colorful art style, and memorable design. You play as a mother and a daughter as you explore the mysterious levels.

The game's artists studied a variety of architecture from around the world, including Spain, Germany, and China.

The artists also took inspiration from sweets and toys. This led to them creating a more colorful world.

The idea was to have each level look so good that you'd want to print the screen and put it on a wall. It worked!

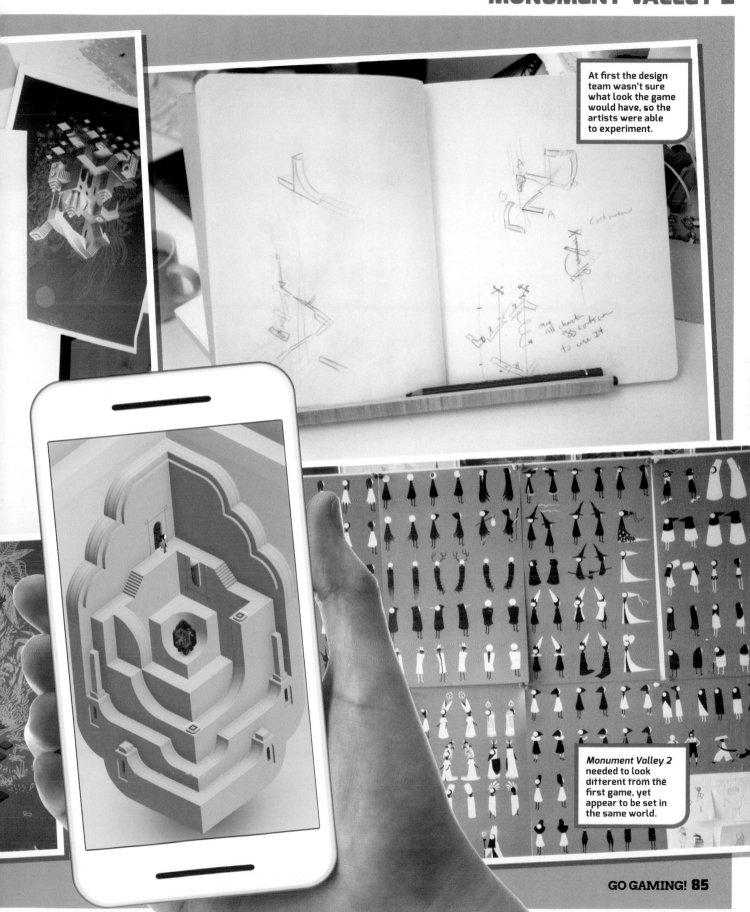

At first the design team wasn't sure what look the game would have, so the artists were able to experiment.

Monument Valley 2 needed to look different from the first game, yet appear to be set in the same world.

THE HARDEST GAMES

WORK HARD, PLAY EVEN HARDER

Many games like to hold you by the hand and give you a little nudge in the right direction whenever you get stuck. That's because a lot of developers are worried that you might give up if things are a bit too challenging and they want to encourage you to continue playing for as long as possible. But what if you want to test your gaming skills to the max? Luckily, you can. Some games pose a fiendish challenge, and here are some of the best you can try. Remember, keep trying. You can always come back to it later if you get stuck.

TRAP ADVENTURE 2

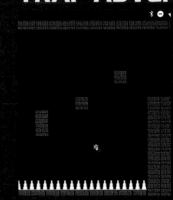

Trap Adventure 2 is a slice of pure genius that will challenge anyone. You have ten lives but you'll soon eat through the lot, and to make matters worse the game laughs when it's game over. But you're sure to love this one.

OUT THERE: Ω EDITION

Time to put on your space helmet because you're about to explore the night sky, visiting planets to find fuel, supplies, and food in a bid to survive. The challenge comes in figuring how best to manage your resources while deciding what you do and don't need.

THE IMPOSSIBLE GAME

The name of this game says it all. Who knew that tapping on your screen to land on the black squares and avoid spikes could be this frustrating? How many attempts will you need to get through all five of this game's deadly levels?

Attempt 17

RISE UP

A quick burst of this game is easy enough, but get farther and you'll be puffing air out of your cheeks. Use your finger to protect a balloon from popping by smashing objects out of the way.

FINAL FANTASY IV

This role-playing game was hard enough when it was first released, and it certainly hasn't gotten much easier. Don't be afraid to ask your parents for help, and stick with it. The rich storytelling and amazing random battles will win you over.

FAST FACT

Final Fantasy IV was known as *Final Fantasy II* in North America when it was first released, and you can also play it on a Nintendo DS.

DUET GAME

Spinning your way through this musical maze requires gut instinct and fast reactions. Once in tune you should have lots of fun. Think of it as a tricky dance using your fingers—and wipe the sweat off your forehead after each level.

PIXEL DUNGEON 2

Pixel Dungeon 2 is referred to as a rogue-like game—a subgenre of RPGs that involves crawling through a dungeon, finding stuff, and battling beasties. In this case, however, even the easy setting is really difficult to master. If you eventually find the Amulet of Yendor, then you have achieved a level of gaming greatness.

VOEZ

Music can make your heart sing but, in the case of the rhythm game *Voez*, it can also make your brain want to scream out loud. Tap, hold, slide, or swipe different notes as they fall to the bottom of the screen and try to be as accurate as you can.

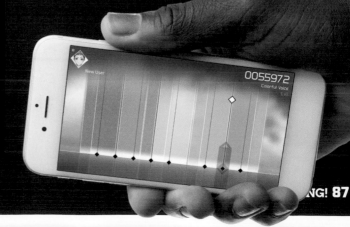

FAST FACT

The first of *Final Fantasy XV: Pocket Edition*'s ten chapters is free. If you like it (and you will) then you can buy the other nine.

TIPS & TRICKS

PARRY & DODGE
When an enemy unleashes a big attack you have the chance to parry or dodge by quickly tapping the icon that appears, so be ready.

SPEND, SPEND, SPEND
Remember to spend the AP you collect to upgrade your stats to make you more effective in battle.

WARP STRIKE
Hold your finger on an enemy to unleash a warp strike. This is a great way of surprising an enemy from a distance.

FINAL FANTASY XV: POCKET EDITION

MAKING A MINI-EPIC

The idea behind *Final Fantasy XV: Pocket Edition* is great: take a huge, big-budget console RPG and reimagine it in a more compact style for a handheld device. Rather than cram the realistic graphics of the main game onto mobile, *Pocket Edition* instead uses its own charming cartoony style, while the game's controls have also been reworked. Finally, there's the story. Gone is the huge open world and long sections of exploration. Instead, *Pocket Edition* pushes you from one exciting story moment to the next, giving the game a sense of pace that's perfect for mobile.

LIKE THIS? ALSO CHECK OUT…

FINAL FANTASY VI
There are lots of classic *Final Fantasy* games that have been re-released on mobile if you want to go back and experience the best games in *Final Fantasy* history. This is one of them.

DISSIDIA FINAL FANTASY: OPERA OMNIA
If you're a *Final Fantasy* fan, this game will be a real treat for you. In *Opera Omnia* you gradually collect a team built from characters taken from throughout *Final Fantasy*'s history.

TOP 5... FEATURES

THE STORY

1 Epic stories have always been a big part of why people love *Final Fantasy* games, and *Pocket Edition* pushes the focus of that element of the game in a big way. You'll meet some great characters and enjoy some amazing moments as you follow it from beginning to end.

BATTLES

2 *Final Fantasy XV: Pocket Edition* keeps the main game's cool weapon-switching system, but makes some great changes that make battles work better on mobile. For example, the game uses an overhead view that makes it easy to see what's going on around you.

CAMARADERIE

3 The relationship between *Final Fantasy XV*'s main characters is one of the great things about its story. Through their long road trips and late-night campfires, which are used to level up after a hard day's fighting, the group builds up a strong, and sometimes hilarious, bond.

SUMMONS

4 *Final Fantasy XV* features some incredible summons—gigantic god-like creatures that show up to attack enemies with powerful abilities. They are always an awe-inspiring sight when they appear in the game's story, towering above everything else around them.

CHOCOBO RIDING

5 Those huge feathered friends that you ride swiftly across the land are one of the iconic sights of the *Final Fantasy* series. Thankfully they return in *Final Fantasy XV: Pocket Edition*, so you get to ride them once again.

FAST FACT

The cameras and takedowns in *Asphalt 9: Legends* were inspired by popular jet fighter games and the ramps and stunts were taken from famous skateboarding games. How's that for a mix of genres!

Thanks to the nitro boosts you earn during races, *Asphalt 9: Legends* can get really, really fast. Don't take your eyes off the road for even a split second!

TIPS & TRICKS

CREATE A CLUB
Creating a club with your friends means you can race together, making a more enjoyable game.

LEARN EACH TRACK
If you're struggling to win races against your friends, practice by yourself. Knowledge is power and the more experienced you are, the better you'll be!

OUTSIDE IN
Remember that for each corner, you want to start on the outside and slow down while driving to the inside of the corner.

ASPHALT 9: LEGENDS

ARE YOU THE FASTEST?

Push your smartphone to breaking point with *Asphalt 9: Legends*, the fastest racing game around. Fearless drivers can take on their friends in eight-player races or you can team up and create your own racing club, challenging others around the world. With the wide range of game modes, awesome soundtrack, and slick graphics, it'll be a long time before you get bored of *Asphalt 9: Legends*.

LIKE THIS? ALSO CHECK OUT…

HILL CLIMB RACING 2
For those who don't want their racing to be serious, give this racer a try. Attempting to control those bouncy vehicles is hilarious fun in multiplayer and sure to cause arguments with your friends!

GRAND PRIX STORY 2
Instead of racing the cars, in this clever game, you are the manager of a Grand Prix team. You have to build cars, hire your staff, and upgrade equipment to win the championship.

THE BATTLE OF POLYTOPIA

CONQUER THE WORLD!

If you've ever felt like you wanted to take over the world, *The Battle of Polytopia* is a good place to start as it gives you tiny video game worlds to conquer. You start off with a single city and then roam the map to find new settlements to join you—or enemies to battle.

Over time you earn money, which can be used to build new units and buildings or research technologies to make your tribe more powerful. The winner is the last tribe standing or whoever has the highest score in the 30-turn "Perfection" mode.

FAST FACT

"Poly-" means many and "-topia" refers to "utopia," meaning many perfect societies in this case.

Late on in a game, multiple battles can break out, and super units stomp about the map with their gigantic swords.

TIPS & TRICKS

START SMALL
Choose fewer opponents and the map is smaller. This is better for learning the game, especially when you select the Easy difficulty level.

EXPAND CITIES
When cities level up, you get a reward. For level 4, choose border growth if there's space around your city, so you have room for more buildings.

GO SUPER
At level 5, you can choose a massive super unit as your prize. Do this when a city's first occupied and your enemy's kicked out!

LIKE THIS? ALSO CHECK OUT...

LETTERPRESS
This game combines both spelling and conquering territory. You use the letters of the words you create to capture and protect your land—and to also make sneak attacks on your opponent's squares.

WARBITS
This cartoonish turn-based war game is set inside a computer. The premise is that if people aren't really fighting each other, the galaxy might be saved. That doesn't mean the missions are easy though!

THE BEST MULTIPLAYER GAMES

FUN WITH FRIENDS

Everything is more fun with friends, and video games are no exception. They can give you that amazing satisfaction of winning together as a team and get you laughing in a way you never would playing on your own. Whether you want to team up with your buddies online, test your skills against each other in a head-to-head matchup, or find a fun party game that can get you all playing together in the same room, we've got you covered with this list of great games.

FORTNITE

The goal of the game is to be the last person or team standing. You get dropped into a map at the beginning and must quickly collect resources to build forts to help you take out enemies. You'll be playing up to 99 other players if you go solo, or you can pair up in a two or compete as a team of four and work together.

FAST FACT

There are 21 unique brawlers for you to unlock and play as in *Brawl Stars*. Can you unlock every single one?

ASPHALT 9: LEGENDS

This arcade racer lets you choose from a list of real-life supercars and take them to the track. The racing itself, however, throws realism out the window in favor of fun. You'll be pulling off huge drifts as you skid through tight streets and flying off massive jumps to send your car spinning through the air.

BRAWL STARS

You can play against your friends or team up to play against teams of other players online in this fun brawler. As you play around in the game's different modes you will unlock new brawlers to play as, each with their own signature attack and super ability.

RIPTIDE GP: RENEGADE

 Mobile tilt controls are a perfect way of capturing the feeling of your rider leaning into the turns. The game does have a solo campaign, but you'll be missing out if you don't experience the excitement of racing in multiplayer.

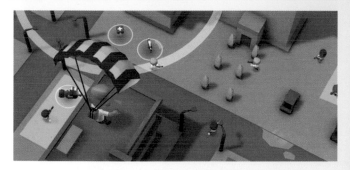

BATTLELANDS ROYALE

 A mobile-focused take on the Battle Royale formula seen in games like *Fortnite*, *Battlelands* focuses on getting you playing quickly in short two- to three-minute affairs, perfect for a quick blast on mobile.

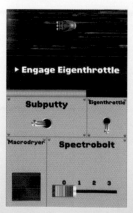

SPACETEAM

 You and your friends are part of a spaceship crew. Each player has a different control panel with buttons and dials labeled with nonsense technobabble. Orders will appear on each player's screen and you all have to shout out the tasks to each other.

JUST DANCE NOW

 Choose from a huge list of great songs and use your phone to track your dancing as you compete to see whose moves can best match the game's dances.

DUAL!

 Playing against a friend using another mobile device, *Dual!* is a game where you shoot at each other from one screen to another—the shots that disappear off the edge of your screen appear on your opponent's, and vice versa. Be ready to dodge!

Lara Croft GO won the Apple iPhone Game of the Year, just one of the many awards this clever puzzle game has to its name. The game was based on *Hitman GO* by the same developers.

Snakes are one of the earliest enemies you'll battle. Make sure you approach them from the side or from behind, where they can't bite you.

LARA CROFT GO

LARA ON THE MOVE

Lara Croft GO is a turn-based puzzle game (starring the famous adventurer) meaning the enemies won't move until you do. Picking a path through the perilous caves and temples will give your brain a good workout. You'll spend just as long studying level layouts and plotting your next move as you will battling snakes and giant spiders.

TIPS & TRICKS

TAKE YOUR TIME
Think ahead. Don't rush because enemies won't move until you do, so use the pause in action to carefully plan out your moves.

LOOK AHEAD
Study each level. Each platform, lever, and item has a purpose, even if it doesn't seem obvious. Figure out how to reach them all.

USE TRIAL AND ERROR
Try moving Lara around to see what happens. Sometimes her movement will set enemies off in surprising ways.

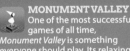

ALSO CHECK OUT…

MONUMENT VALLEY
One of the most successful games of all time, *Monument Valley* is something everyone should play. Its relaxing gameplay meshes perfectly with its beautiful artwork.

GHOSTS OF MEMORIES
This gorgeous game is definitely for those who want a challenge. With physics-based puzzles and tricky platforms to explore, you'll have to think outside the box to get to the end.

RAYMAN ADVENTURES

JUST KEEP RUNNING

Rayman may not have any arms or legs, but that doesn't prevent him from zipping all over the place in this awesome auto-running 2-D platformer. Guide the game's hero through seven worlds and over 200 different levels while collecting Lums, rescuing Teensies, and collecting Ancient Eggs to re-grow the Sacred Tree. You can also unlock unique helpers called Incrediballs, little creatures that aid you on your quest by pointing out treasure, attracting special items, and shielding you from enemy attacks. The best part? All the graphics are hand-painted, so it feels like you're playing an incredible work of art!

TIPS & TRICKS

WHO'S HUNGRY?
In order to continue using your Incrediballs, you need to keep them full and happy. Feed them after every stage.

GOTTA CATCH 'EM ALL!
Find and incubate Ancient Eggs by completing levels and freeing them from their cages.

BEST TOOL FOR THE JOB
There are three different types of Incrediball: Inhalers, Protectors, and Seekers. Match your buddy to the current level icon for the best results.

FAST FACT

Rayman Adventures is the third mobile *Rayman* game, after both *Rayman Jungle Run* and *Rayman Fiesta Run*. The series dates back to 1995 and features 44 different games across many platforms.

LIKE THIS? ALSO CHECK OUT…

BADLAND 2
Play as fuzzy flying creature Clone and flap your way through spooky and desolate alien environments in this shadowy 2-D obstacle game. Avoid countless dangers if you can!

LEO'S FORTUNE
Help blue fluff-ball Leopold hunt down his lost gold fortune in this stunning 2-D exploration game. There are 24 levels of mind-bending puzzles and treacherous traps.

FAST FACT

Chuchel was created by Amanita Design, a Czech-based indie developer. Chuchel, the name of the game's main hero, is a Czech word that literally means "ball of hair and dust."

The game begins with Chuchel fast asleep. Guess what? You have to wake him up! Maybe some cold water will get him out of bed . . .

CHUCHEL

IT'S ONE OF A KIND

Sure, sometimes video games can get really weird. But seriously, there's nothing out there quite like *Chuchel*. In this totally bizarre point-and-click adventure by the makers of *Samorost* and *Botanicula*, you control one of the wackiest main characters of all time—a goofy ball of grime and soot who has only one goal: to track down and hold onto his prized cherry. The big problem is that a giant hairy hand keeps stealing it away, so you need to solve puzzles and meet crazy characters to help your silly friend get it back.

TIPS & TRICKS

MAN'S BEST FRIEND
Kekel is Chuchel's tiny purple pet. Sometimes it will steal the cherry, while other times it can actually help you out with solving puzzles.

JUST KEEP TRYING
If you get stuck in one of *Chuchel*'s 30 different levels, look for the signpost with a question mark on it. Tap it and a helpful hint will appear.

FLAPPY BIRD
During the flying stage, tap to make Chuchel rise up into the air and stop to make him fall. Dodge all the jumping creatures to move on.

LIKE THIS? ALSO CHECK OUT . . .

HIDDEN FOLKS
Jump into a miniature world filled to the brim with charming hand-drawn black-and-white drawings. Hilarious animation and sound effects make this *Where's Waldo?*-style hidden object game really worth checking out.

LITTLE BRIAR ROSE
This enchanting fairytale point-and-click adventure is based on the Brothers Grimm and Disney classic *Sleeping Beauty*. But here's the best part: the unique graphics featured throughout look just like stained-glass window art.

POCKET CITY

MAKE YOUR OWN METROPOLIS

It takes a lot of time, money, and hard work to build a flourishing real-life city from scratch, but in *Pocket City*, getting started is as simple as swiping your finger to build roads, houses, factories, and more. *Pocket City* re-imagines the classic *SimCity* formula for touch devices, making it absorbingly easy to assemble your ideal urban metropolis. Luckily, there's also plenty of depth within, as you'll need to keep residents happy, manage traffic, provide resources, and even respond to natural disasters along the way.

TIPS & TRICKS

MIND THE STATS
The Stats tab is your key to a healthy, thriving city: it shows strengths and weaknesses, as well as citizen demands.

UTILIZE UTILITIES
You can't just drop power plants and water towers anywhere: see how far they reach on the map to make sure all buildings are well served.

TAP TO REBUILD
If your city is demolished after a natural disaster, go to Report in the Events tab to find the option to restore your construction.

66 Testington

$410,000

15,867

Aaah!

FAST FACT

Pocket City has zero in-app purchases, so you can't pay your way through timers or roadblocks, or spend for special perks.

Maybe constructing a city around that active volcano wasn't the best idea. Oh well, time to rebuild!

VIEW▲   STATS   BUILD   QUESTS   EVENTS

LIKE THIS? ALSO CHECK OUT...

SIMCITY BUILDIT
The official *SimCity* mobile experience is flashier than *Pocket City* and packs in real-world landmarks and multiplayer elements. However, the free-to-play model can be frustrating.

MINECRAFT
It's a very different kind of experience, but *Minecraft* lets you get hands-on as you construct a building or entire city, block by block. This is an essential game for any mobile player.

THE BEST BRAIN GAMES

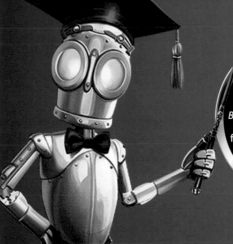

PUT YOUR MIND TO WORK

We can learn so much from video games. Whether building huge structures in *Minecraft* or exploring the outside world with *Pokémon GO*, there's always something putting our minds to the test. If you want to exercise your brain even further, there are plenty of games designed to do just that. So when you feel like learning a new skill or simply improving your knowledge in a fun and creative way, this list is for you.

FAST FACT

Brain Wars and *Brain Dots* were made by Translimit. The former has been downloaded over 20 million times, while the latter has 35 million downloads.

BRAIN WARS

Brain Wars lets you challenge like-minded friends and players online in real-time brainteaser battles, focusing on tasks such as concentration and matching exercises.

JUST RIDDLES

There are lots of brainteasers to solve in *Just Riddles*, which provides small clues to help you find the right answers. They're fun, quick, and not too difficult to complete, but if you find yourself struggling you can spend the coins you earn on helpful hints.

COMIC LIFE 3

Some brain games are less about testing your mind and more about letting it run wild. *Comic Life 3* is just that—your very own comic book creator that works with the photos on your phone. With this game, you can turn yourself into the ultimate superhero!

LIGHTBOT: CODE HOUR

 If you're interested in learning how to make video games, this is a great first step. *Lightbot* introduces you to the basics of coding, and although it won't teach you how to make a game outright, you'll get an idea of how programming concepts such as commands and loops work.

SLICE FRACTIONS 2

 Learning math isn't always easy and it can also be a bore from time-to-time. *Slice Fractions 2* is a great way of having fun while learning key skills, featuring over 100 puzzles designed to help you get to grips with the basics of fractions. The story centers around a cute mammoth that is desperate to retrieve his stolen hat. The graphics are detailed and eye-catching throughout each of the game's three worlds. When you're finished, you might even want to go back and try the original game, which won multiple awards back in 2014.

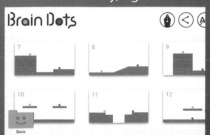

BRAIN DOTS

 There are two colored dots on the screen. Your job is to draw a path to make them bump together. Sounds easy, right? It's not so simple—the level of difficulty gets harder over the 300+ stages, and you'll need to use smart thinking to complete them all.

A CLOCKWORK BRAIN

 *A Clockwork Brain* is a typical brain-training game in which you're tasked with completing various challenges. There are loads of puzzles testing everything from your memory to your language skills, and you can track your performance stats as you go. The best part about the game is how visually impressive it is, highlighted by a friendly robot called Sprocket who guides you through the game's collection of levels. You can even use special "Petbots" to help give you a helping hand when you need it, and each one of these mechanical animals boasts its own unique traits.

QUICK BRAIN

 Quick Brain is another great math game which focuses on adding, subtracting, multiplying, and dividing. It challenges you to complete each task as quickly as possible to increase your score.

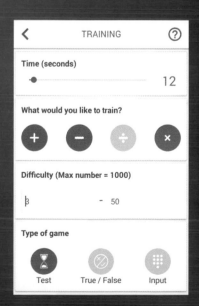

Now I see why this was listed as a **charming fixer-upper!**

Your first house isn't much to look at, but you can turn it into a cozy home in no time.

FAST FACT

The other *Sims* game on mobile is *The Sims Freeplay*, developed by Firemonkeys Studios and first released in 2011. But unlike *Freeplay*, *The Sims Mobile* is closer to the original PC series of games.

THE SIMS MOBILE

THE GAME OF LIFE

For the better part of two decades, fans have been acting out the lives of their virtual Sims in EA's long-running series. *The Sims Mobile* allows you to create your own characters, build their houses, and even manage their careers as you progress through the story. The amount of activities and customization options on offer is huge, and there's real scope to let your imagination truly run wild. It's completely free to download, too, so you needn't pay a thing to get started.

TIPS & TRICKS

CLEAR YOUR SCHEDULE
Your "Daily To Do List" is the best way to earn loads of in-game rewards, including XP and Simoleons.

SAVE YOUR CASH
It's tempting to spend your SimCash early in the game, but you'll need it more later, so save up as much as possible.

BE SURE TO SOCIALIZE
Grow your relationships with the Sims around you. That way, you'll open up new story options while earning rewards.

LIKE THIS? ALSO CHECK OUT...

SIMCITY BUILDIT
If you'd rather design and monitor a city than its inhabitants, *SimCity Buildit* is the simulation game for you. Build your very own neighborhood and take on others in the Contest of Mayors!

ROLLERCOASTER TYCOON CLASSIC
Combining the best bits of this famous series' first two outings, this game allows you to build your own theme park, complete with crazy rollercoaster track designs.

SUPERBROTHERS: SWORD & SWORCERY EP

AN ENCHANTING, ECCENTRIC ADVENTURE

Superbrothers: Sword & Sworcery EP is an odd name, but it's also a rather peculiar game. This role-playing adventure is punctuated by ultra-minimal pixel graphics, an experimental indie rock soundtrack, offbeat and hilarious writing, and a combat system that requires you to rotate your phone to begin swinging your sword! But it all comes together beautifully, delivering one of the most captivating, one-of-a-kind experiences you can play on a smartphone. Get comfy, plug in some headphones, and lose yourself in this quirky quest.

TIPS & TRICKS

USE THE MEGATOME
You'll eventually uncover the "Megatome," a magical book that's packed with little details and nuggets of info. Flip through it for tips if you get stuck.

THE SHIELD HEALS
Combat can be tricky, but the shield does more than just block attacks. Hold down the icon for a few seconds and you'll recover some health.

FUMBLE YOUR PHONE
Some perplexing puzzles can be solved by rotating or shaking your phone, or swiping and tapping in some unexpected way. Experiment (carefully) with your device!

An enormous mountain shaped like a bearded man's head, and you can enter through the mouth? Yeah, that's Sword & Sworcery EP's unique style.

FAST FACT

Sword & Sworcery's critically acclaimed soundtrack, composed by Canadian singer-songwriter Jim Guthrie, is called The Ballad of the Space Babies and led to Jim soundtracking a documentary.

LIKE THIS? ALSO CHECK OUT...

MONUMENT VALLEY 2
Monument Valley 2 is a memorable quest that sees you guiding Ro and her child through a series of perplexing yet stunning levels. Rotate towers, twist knobs, and overcome visually confounding obstacles to reach each goal.

FEZ
Fez looks like an old-school game in a classic Super Mario sort of way, but there's a big twist: the supposedly 2-D world can be rotated 90 degrees, revealing new pathways and secrets as you navigate this surreal jaunt.

DRAGON HILLS 2

RIP-ROARING RUNNER FUN

The next time your parents tell you to stop making a mess, launch this game and do your worst. With *Dragon Hills 2*, destruction really is the name of the game as you ride a beast through a world of zombies and look to smash everything in sight. For maximum carnage you need to tunnel deep into the ground before launching into the sky with speed and power. This lets you defeat enemies, cut through buildings, and send vehicles flying into the air. Gaming is rarely so satisfying.

TIPS & TRICKS

SMASH THROUGH BUILDINGS
You can't stay underground for too long but try and time your moves so that you come back up beneath a building to soar even higher into the air.

DON'T GET SLIMED
Slime will hurt you so the best way to avoid it is to look ahead and decide whether it's easier to jump over or tunnel under.

SLOW THE DRAGON
In the boss battles look for the precise moment slime is thrown your way and immediately duck. Lots of diving and surfacing causes your dragon to speed up, too.

You can get through the entire game by just tapping the screen at the right moments, making it simple to learn but hard to master.

FAST FACT

There are many unlockables in *Dragon Hills 2* so collect gold coins and boost your dragon's abilities: they may help in the game's fiendish boss battles.

LIKE THIS? ALSO CHECK OUT...

SUPER MEGA WORM
Just like *Dragon Hills 2*, this retro-styled game lets you travel underground and high into the air. But the action involves a hungry worm that wants to eat humans and destroy their machines and robots. Eek!

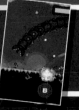

DEATH WORM
There are some deep similarities between this game and *Dragon Hills 2*. But instead of one-tap play, you need to move the hungry monster underground using an on-screen controller. Smash cars, tanks, and UFOs.

FAST FACT

According to the developer Blowfish Studios, *Morphite* was inspired by classic console games including *Ratchet & Clank* and *Metroid Prime*.

You view the game from a first-person perspective and this makes you feel far more involved in the near non-stop action.

MORPHITE
OLD TIMER RETURNS TO EPICNESS

Fancy a jaunt around space? Then climb aboard *Morphite* and you can soon get going. This game lets you fly from one planet to another in a bid to gather vital resources. But, as is often the case, you will also be called upon to defend yourself and your ship against various nasties so you need to keep your wits about you. Most of the game feels like a first-person shooter (FPS) yet there are puzzles to solve and a story to get stuck into. It's like having a console game in the palm of your hands.

TIPS & TRICKS

STOCKPILE BOMBS
You will need as many bombs as you can get your hands on as you explore the planets and seek to open fresh ways forward. Seek them out at all times.

ALTER THE CONTROLS
Tap the pause button during play, select Settings and choose the Control tab. You can now alter the sensitivity of the controls and movement to suit your style of play.

JUST KEEP SCANNING
The game's tutorial tells you to shoot everything if you're unsure what to do but you should scan all plants, creatures, and other items, too, to unlock upgrades and money.

ALSO CHECK OUT...

OUT THERE: Ω EDITION
This is another game of survival based in the outer reaches of space. *Out There* has you drifting alone in a space cruiser and needing to visit planets to collect mineral supplies, fuel, and oxygen while uncovering secrets along the way.

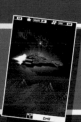

BEYOND SPACE REMASTERED
This 3-D space blaster puts the universe at your disposal. There's a *Star Wars* vibe about it because it touches on conflict and politics, and it provides the perfect backdrop for the ensuing action.

ESSENTIAL ACCESSORIES

TRANSFORM YOUR GAMING EXPERIENCE

It's easier than ever to turn your mobile device into a fully-fledged games console. As you've no doubt seen in this wonderful book, the quality and range of games available to you while on the move only continues to grow—so why not improve the experience by bringing some accessories into the mix? Here we have cataloged what we believe to be the essential peripherals to make playing video games on your phone even more comfortable and enjoyable than you ever thought possible.

A CONTROLLER ADD-ON

Do you like the look of the Nintendo Switch but haven't been able to get your hands on one? Why not try a controller that connects directly to your smartphone. Designed to wrap around your device, these controllers offer full gamepad support to your mobile and feature analog sticks, a D-pad, and a range of face buttons. They give you more precision and flexibility on some of the very best games available to you on mobile. They also connect via the charging port on your phone so won't use up all of your battery through Bluetooth like many other mobile controllers.

A VR HEADSET

There are a host of epic VR games available on mobile and plenty of incredible VR headsets to choose from, too, no matter what smartphone you own. So choose one that fits your budget, hook it up to your phone, get yourself a Bluetooth controller, and prepare for a truly excellent VR gaming experience.

GAMING HEADPHONES

No mobile gaming setup would be complete without a high-quality pair of headphones. Helping to immerse you in the gaming action, there are a number of options available to you that offer an awesome sound, a mic for multiplayer voice chat, and, thanks to their 3.5mm jack inputs, will work with almost any device!

A BATTERY POWER PACK

As you probably know, gaming on the go will *destroy* your battery. That's why you are going to want a power pack if you're serious about mobile gaming. This handy device powers up your phone and will give most phones four whole extra charges— perfect for long car journeys, camping, or for days away from home.

A PRO CONTROLLER

There are several incredible accessories that can transform gaming on the go. Here are six that gaming dreams are made of. Some controllers can secure your phone in a cradle to help you find the optimum position for playing while on the move. A pro controller will turn your smartphone into a true handheld console, supporting all of the biggest games and making them more comfortable to play. If you enjoy games such as *Fortnite* or *Vainglory*, a serious controller could help you move up the leaderboards in no time.

RETRO WIRELESS CONTROLLER

This will make your parents feel old! There are retro-themed controllers for iOS or Android devices. You can play on near-perfect re-creations of iconic controllers from yesteryear, and make any retro game you're playing feel even more authentic.

A TRADITIONAL-STYLE GAMEPAD

If you're looking for a gaming experience on your phone that feels as good as a PS4 or Xbox One controller, then try one of these traditional-style gamepads. Combine one with VR or Chromecast to create a truly epic home console experience.

A STYLUS

For games that aren't fast-paced you may want to think about using a stylus for your screen. It won't leave fingerprints, your presses can be more accurate, and your hand won't get in the way of the action. Many companies make these gadgets and they come in different sizes and styles, so you can pick what's best for you.

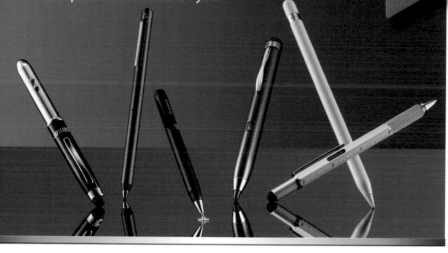

A BUDGET OPTION

If you have an iOS or Android device, a cardboard VR headset is one of the best ways that you can experience virtual reality gaming. While they may look and feel pretty basic, the tradeoff is that they're cheap to buy! If you've never had a VR experience before, this is the perfect way to get started.

A STREAMING DEVICE

Want to take your favorite mobile games off your little Android or iOS phone screen and play them on the TV? Google Chromecast (either the basic or ultra variants), use your home's WiFi connection to stream games from your phone right to your TV!

FAST FACT

The very first *Command & Conquer* came out in 1995, making it one of the longest-running series in gaming. One of the first ever real-time strategy game franchises, it was based on *Dune II*.

TIPS & TRICKS

GO QUICKLY
Getting your buildings up and running before the other player gives you a huge advantage.

AVOID POINTLESS FIGHTS
Once you have a small army built up, you'll think you can catch the other player out, but losing an early fight will almost certainly lose you the game.

CHECK DAILY CHALLENGES
Unlock massive rewards by completing the daily challenges, so make it a habit to check when you log in. Every reward helps!

COMMAND & CONQUER: RIVALS

LET BATTLE COMMENCE

If you're as fast with your brain as you are with your thumbs, then *Command & Conquer: Rivals* is your perfect game. Race against your opponent to build the biggest army and gain victory. You need to find the right mix of infantry, tanks, and aircraft, spending your resources wisely as you assemble an awesome battalion. You will also need to establish a base of operations, deciding whether to split your resources between your army or your buildings. Can you survive a battle against your friends?

LIKE THIS? ALSO CHECK OUT…

GALAXY REAVERS
Spaceships come together to do battle in the farthest reaches of the galaxy in this strategy title. Action-packed, it will light up your mobile with bright lasers and fiery explosions.

RYMDKAPSEL
In this mysterious sci-fi strategy game, you have to build up your spaceport to defend it from invaders. It's unlike anything else you'll ever play, while still delivering intense strategic action.

SILLY WALKS

PLAY WITH YOUR FOOD

What's wackier than a bowl of noodles traversing a dangerous kitchen gauntlet of meat tenderizers and flaming burners? Very little—which is why *Silly Walks* is such a hilarious treat. It puts you in the shoes (yes, shoes) of a doughnut, a pizza slice, or a popcorn box as you try to conquer kitchen obstacle courses and rescue your fellow food pals from an evil blender. Each tap guides your clumsy snack hero a single step forward. As fun to play as it is to watch.

TIPS & TRICKS

DO THE DASH
Most of the time, you'll tap to move each leg along—but a well-timed swipe will quickly dash you ahead. Just avoid dashing off the edge.

FINISH MISSIONS
Each level has bonus missions—like kicking cups or collecting candy—that award extra sugar cubes, which you can use to unlock new food heroes.

SPEED UP
Safe and steady movement is smart, but you can also quickly blast through an area by rapidly tapping the screen. Again, make sure you use it carefully!

It's all just an average day for a donut: dodging killer kitchen implements and kicking over soda cans in a mad dash along the counter.

LIKE THIS? ALSO CHECK OUT...

PLANTS VS. ZOMBIES
This wonderfully weird strategy game pits common garden plants against undead invaders, as you wield pea-shooters and explosive potato mines to repel the waves of backyard attackers. PopCap's enduring favorite is still a blast.

BAG IT!
Eager to play games with yet more food? *Bag It!* tasks you with stacking cartoonish groceries into a sack, challenging you to find the ideal fit for everything without crushing any of your goods in the process. It's trickier than it sounds!

Things become more complicated when enemy creatures become involved, making timing all-important if you want to complete a stage.

SPLITTER CRITTERS

SPLICE UP THE WORLD

Splitter Critters is perfect for touchscreen devices, allowing you to slash the playing area into pieces with your finger, then rearrange them so the aliens can reach their UFO and escape to the next level. It's also a wonderfully perplexing puzzler full of hazards, enemy creatures to avoid, and multiple ways to complete a stage. Add in aliens that react in different ways and you'll find it hard to put down.

TIPS & TRICKS

WATCH THE ALIENS
The different colored aliens have their own patterns of movement and behavior, so watch them carefully.

KEEP UNDOING
You are only allowed to make three cuts to the screen at any one time, so learn how to use the undo button to your advantage.

GET HINTS
If you become stuck on a level for too long, a hint button will appear in the bottom-right corner. Press it for a suggested move.

LIKE THIS? ALSO CHECK OUT...

KIWANUKA
The main focus of Kiwanuka is a magician and his friends whom you need to guide to an exit across some very weird and wonderful levels. You do this by dragging a magic rod and creating towers.

ANTS
The aim here is to get your ants to climb, build steps, parachute, dig, and get themselves across water in order to find safety at the end of each level. It's very Lemmings-like.

SPACE PIONEER

SPACE-BASED SHARP SHOOTER

The first top-down blaster was *Galaxian* in 1979, but the genre remains as fresh as ever. This is proven by the beautiful-looking *Space Pioneer*, which puts you in the shoes of a bounty hunter in hot pursuit of a bad guy named Xeldar. As you explore different planets and try to defeat him, you have to battle against hordes of enemy aliens and complete many fun objectives.

TIPS & TRICKS

GRAB A HEALTH PACK
Before you begin a mission on a new planet, select a health pack. You will find a good use for it.

DON'T FIRE CONSTANTLY
You may be tempted to run around with your finger on the fire button, but this overheats your weapon.

BUILD YOUR BASE
Once you unlock the base feature, make good use of it to create everything you can, from workshops to an armory to a crystals generator.

MAIN OBJECTIVES

KILL ALL ENEMIES

FAST FACT

The environments within the game are procedurally generated, which means the computer creates them, allowing for an infinite number of planets.

LIKE THIS? ALSO CHECK OUT...

PIXEL CRAFT – SPACE SHOOTER
This retro arcade top-down blaster has the simplest of controls: just swipe around the screen and the craft will automatically fire on any oncoming enemies. Running at speed, it's a game with bags of energy.

CRASHLANDS
In this top-down action game based in space your task is to survive, and much time is spent battling against enemies. It's not a frantic game like *Space Pioneer*, but you'll go on an adventure for sure.

THE BEST ESPORTS GAMES

GET YOUR GAME ON

Competitive gaming is bigger and more exciting than ever, with plenty of huge console and PC games drawing top-skilled players, millions of viewers, and even millions of dollars in prize pools. Mobile games are getting in on the eSports fun, too, with international competitions for team-based action games, competitive card games, and other thrilling multiplayer experiences. Here's a look at the best eSports games you can play on your smartphone today. Can you become the next great champion?

VAINGLORY 5v5

This gorgeous fantasy game is a team-based tactical brawler, tasking opposing five-player teams with toppling the other's turrets and base to secure the Vain crystal. *Vainglory* is one of mobile's longest-running eSports, thanks to a level of strategic depth that rivals PC games plus a robust international scene of skilled players.

FAST FACT

When it was first released *Vainglory* was a 3v3 game, but it was recently upgraded to 5v5 and given a larger map packed full of exciting new strategic possibilities.

ARENA OF VALOR

Like *Vainglory*, *Arena of Valor* is a 5-on-5 strategic action affair that sees teams wield fantastical heroes to try and take down the opposing base . . . plus you can play as Batman and Wonder Woman. *Arena of Valor* has a huge eSports scene in China, and it's now expanding out internationally.

Preyta • Butterfly • Batman • Murad
Toro • Omega • Yorn • Maloch

FORTNITE

Battle royale sensation *Fortnite* is the biggest thing in video games right now, and this free-to-play game plays just the same on smartphones as it does on consoles and PC. It's a 100-player fight to see who will be the last one standing at the end, but *Fortnite* is about more than just well-timed shots and grenade lobs: you can also quickly build structures to protect yourself, reach new heights, or confuse rivals.

HEARTHSTONE

Hearthstone is an immensely popular digital card game that lets you build powerful decks from more than 1,500 cards based on Blizzard's *Warcraft* series. You'll then use them to outwit and outclass opponents in turn-based battles. One of the most popular eSports games around.

WORLD OF TANKS BLITZ

World of Tanks Blitz packs squad-based tank shootouts into bite-sized, mobile-friendly battles, with 7v7 fights between an array of heavily customizable vehicles. Success requires teamwork and tenacity as you try to surprise foes and dominate with cannon shots; unsurprisingly, that makes for exciting competition.

FAST FACT

The Elder Scrolls: Legends is free to play, and there are three expansion packs available to download— *Heroes of Skyrim*, *Return to Clockwork City*, and *Houses of Morrowind*.

POWER RANGERS: LEGACY WARS

After 25 years, *Power Rangers* is still going strong—and *Power Rangers: Legacy Wars* is a treat for fans. This head-to-head fighter lets you command rangers from across the franchise, including the recent film, and features real online competition against other players. Can you become the most powerful ranger of them all?

THE ELDER SCROLLS: LEGENDS

Like the *Elder Scrolls* role-playing epics more than *Warcraft*? If so, then you might pick *Legends* over *Hearthstone*; the card-battlers share similarities, but *The Elder Scrolls: Legends* uses a compelling dual-lane battlefield for cards, plus it benefits from the fascinating *Elder Scrolls* universe.

SUMMONERS WAR

Summoners War takes a slower pace to its strategic action, pitting two players against each other in turn-based, role-playing duels. You'll use each fantasy fighter's special abilities to try and dominate your opponent—and still have heroes left standing at the end. It takes brains and brawn to win this war.

SURVIVAL ARENA

Tower-defense games are typically single-player experiences, but *Survival Arena* turns it into a head-to-head battle: each player must build mazes of defensive turrets to protect his or her base, but also send out attacking units to try and topple the rival's fortifications. It's a clever twist on a familiar theme.

CLASH ROYALE

Clash Royale merges tactical action with strategic deck-building for one of the liveliest competitive experiences found on a touchscreen today. You'll build a small deck full of warriors, mages, goblins, and more, and then enter battle to try and topple your rival's base by dropping characters onto the map. Naturally, the other player is doing the exact same thing, and the resulting skirmishes are not only a blast to play but fun to watch. The Crown Championship tournament awarded $1 million in prizes in 2017, with a new *Clash Royale League* drawing the best battlers.

FAST FACT

Reach over 4,000 trophies in *Clash Royale* and you'll be entered into one of nine different leagues. Players can earn rewards based on league performance each season.

DISNEY HEROES: BATTLE MODE

THE ULTIMATE MASH-UP

What's better than a game featuring characters from *The Incredibles* and *Toy Story*? One that includes both and then adds heroes from *Wreck-It Ralph*, *Zootopia*, and *Pirates of the Caribbean* to the pile! *Disney Heroes: Battle Mode* brings together famous faces from recent Disney and Pixar flicks in a team-based brawler, which sees them facing off against computer virus-infected foes in a digital world. Harness the unique abilities of each character to build the ultimate team, with plenty of upgrades and cool gear boosting your power over time.

TIPS & TRICKS

PLAY REGULARLY
Disney Heroes provides up to five free gold crates to unlock each day, so be sure to log in every so often to nab new heroes and helpful items.

UPGRADE SKILLS
Check in on your heroes regularly to equip perk-packing badges and upgrade your skills. This will boost your ability to dominate in battle.

ENTER THE PORT
"Play in The Port" provides a daily battle challenge that nets you either free experience-boosting drinks or stashes of in-game gold.

 136   2/3   1m 29s

Your super-powered battle squad can take down early foes with ease, but you'll need upgrades and new abilities to face the tougher later challenges.

FAST FACT

More Disney heroes will be added over time, with Kevin Flynn and Quorra from *Tron: Legacy* already joining the fray since the release. Moana and Belle are also planned to be added soon.

LIKE THIS? ALSO CHECK OUT...

 MARVEL STRIKE FORCE
This team-based brawler brings together all sorts of heroes from across the Marvel comics and film universe, including Spider-Man, Iron Man, The Wasp, and Wolverine. Build your squad and repel the evil foes!

 NINJA TURTLES: LEGENDS
Ninja Turtles: Legends lets you experience both sides of the *Teenage Mutant Ninja Turtles* conflict, whether you field a group of well-equipped turtles or command villains like Bebop and Rocksteady against The Kraang.

FAST FACT

RuneScape first began life as an internet browser-based MMORPG way back in 2001, making it even older than *World of Warcraft*.

RUNESCAPE

MMORPG GOES SMALL

RuneScape is one of the biggest massive multiplayer online role playing games (MMORPGs) ever made, and now it's coming to mobile! Developer Jagex has somehow squeezed the titanic game onto mobile without any compromises, perfectly replicating the gameplay and the size of *RuneScape* on the small screen. While there are plenty of MMORPGs available on mobile, nothing matches the scope, the size, or the history of this adventure. With its endless updates and huge playerbase, there's always something new to do and see in *RuneScape*, so grab your sword, staff, or bow and get out there and explore.

TIPS & TRICKS

PLAY WITH FRIENDS
MMORPGs are more fun with friends. Not only are you guaranteed a party to play with, but it means you can pick the right role for the team.

TRY DIFFERENT ROLES
There are three basic roles in *RuneScape* known as Tank (defense), DPS (attack), and Healer (healing). Try all three and see which you prefer.

EXPLORE EVERYWHERE
If you can't beat enemies in a certain area, explore somewhere else. The world is enormous!

LIKE THIS? ALSO CHECK OUT...

ARCANE LEGENDS
One of the oldest MMORPGs on mobile, *Arcane Legends* has stuck around because of its cool co-op play player-versus-player modes. It's easy to pick up and play and the combat is thrilling fun.

CAT QUEST
Despite its simple looks, *Cat Quest* is a large RPG featuring over 50 dungeons and an open world to explore. Defeat enemies, complete quests, and discover tons of exciting gear.

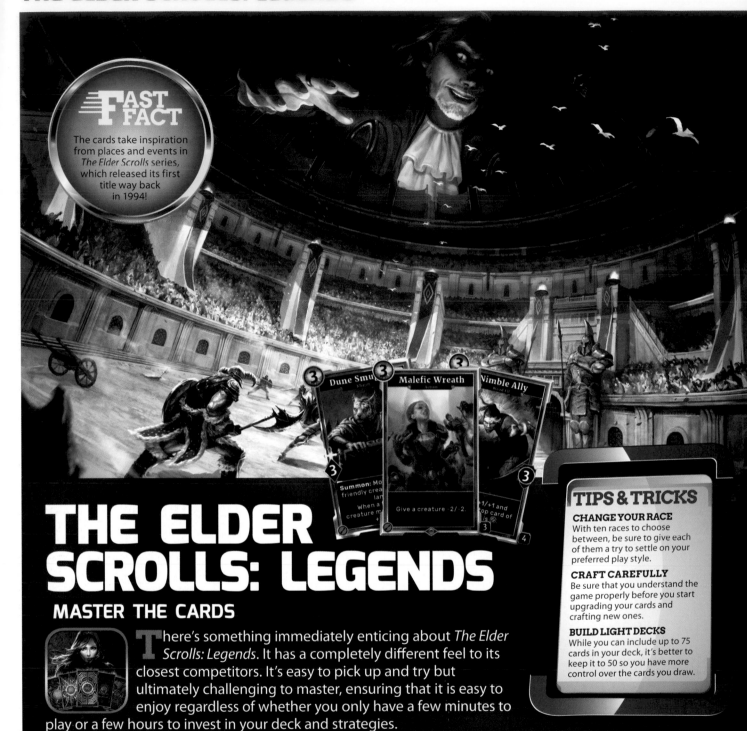

FAST FACT

The cards take inspiration from places and events in *The Elder Scrolls* series, which released its first title way back in 1994!

TIPS & TRICKS

CHANGE YOUR RACE
With ten races to choose between, be sure to give each of them a try to settle on your preferred play style.

CRAFT CAREFULLY
Be sure that you understand the game properly before you start upgrading your cards and crafting new ones.

BUILD LIGHT DECKS
While you can include up to 75 cards in your deck, it's better to keep it to 50 so you have more control over the cards you draw.

THE ELDER SCROLLS: LEGENDS

MASTER THE CARDS

There's something immediately enticing about *The Elder Scrolls: Legends*. It has a completely different feel to its closest competitors. It's easy to pick up and try but ultimately challenging to master, ensuring that it is easy to enjoy regardless of whether you only have a few minutes to play or a few hours to invest in your deck and strategies.

LIKE THIS? ALSO CHECK OUT...

HEARTHSTONE
One of the most popular card games, *Hearthstone* is a card battling game suitable for beginner and intermediate players, with all of its cards based on the *World of Warcraft* universe.

MAGIC DUELS
Never had a chance to play *Magic: The Gathering*? *Magic Duels* is an entry into that competitive card game world, a safe space to learn cards and hone your skills.

FAST FACT

Just want to mess around? *Poly Bridge* has a cool sandbox mode that lets you play around without any restrictions, giving you more freedom to just play.

TIPS & TRICKS

USE THE LINE TRACER
Use the line tracer (or arc tool) to easily trace arcs and straight lines. Joints are automatically snapped on to the curve.

SLOW IT DOWN
To better see which bridge parts are buckling, switch to the 3-D isometric view, tap the stress visibility button and move the right-side slider down.

STAY UNDER BUDGET
Wood is cheaper than steel and you can ensure your structures are strong by forming triangles.

POLY BRIDGE

BRIDGING A GAMING GAP

A game about building bridges sounds boring, right? But get over that initial reaction and this puzzler will really connect with you. All you have to do is construct a road from one side of a river to another. You'll soon discover that it's much trickier than it sounds. Test your handiwork and you may find the bridge collapses, sending vehicles splashing into the water. If so, it's back to the drawing board to strengthen your construction while staying within your budget. How crazy can you make it?

LIKE THIS? ALSO CHECK OUT...

BRIDGE CONSTRUCTOR STUNTS
Another physics-based puzzle game, the difference is that you're encouraged to build daredevil ramps and loops before driving vehicles over them yourself.

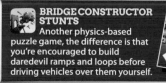

BRIDGE CONSTRUCTION SIM
This game aims to be realistic. As well as using accurate physics it has detailed graphics. You will be tasked with building bridges in cities and valleys.

SHOWCASE

CHUCHEL

Chuchel follows a little ball of dust as he tries to find his cherry that has been stolen. You solve puzzles by doing bizarre and funny things to reach the cherry in each level. *Chuchel* is a very silly game, and there are spoofs of other classic games such as *Tetris* and *Pac-Man*. It is one of the closest things to an interactive cartoon you can get on your mobile device.

The game has a hand-drawn look, and that's because the levels started as sketches, as shown here.

The backgrounds were originally detailed but later made blank to keep the focus on Chuchel and what he was doing.

Characters were drawn in Photoshop, cut out, and then animated, just like how cartoons are made.

These images show the evolution of the game's fourth level. You can see how the game's look changed over time to a more minimalist design.

Chuchel's design changed several times during the game's production. The one in the black hat (right) was the first, but it wasn't originally meant to be used in a game.

THE BEST CROSS-PLATFORM GAMES

PLAY WITH YOUR FRIENDS

Isn't it annoying when you want to play some games with your friends but they have a different phone than you and so it doesn't work? Yeah, it's a huge pain. Thankfully there are some pretty amazing games available that work regardless, letting you play against or alongside your buddies no matter the device they hold in their hand. Behold, the very best cross-platform games for your consideration.

FORTNITE: BATTLE ROYALE

There's no debating it, *Fortnite: Battle Royale* is the biggest competitive multiplayer game in the world. That, aside from the fact that the game is awesome, is largely because of its excellent cross-platform support. If you're playing on iOS or Android you can still link up with your buddies on PC, Switch, and Xbox One.

FAST FACT
You can carry your progression and stats over from *Fortnite* on your phone to another platform, should you choose to do so.

VAINGLORY

Vainglory is purposefully designed to let Android and iOS owners face off. This free-to-play action battler plays wonderfully and, thanks to the cross-platform support, ensures that the servers are always bustling with people to play with and against.

REAL RACING 3

Real Racing 3's innovative time-shifted multiplayer design means that you'll always have other players to race against. It constantly keeps a record of your laps before pushing them out into the world for others to face.

CLASH ROYALE

Clash Royale is one of the most entertaining competitive games on mobile. It's a game with strategy at the heart of it, perfect for cross-platform play.

MINECRAFT: POCKET EDITION

Minecraft is arguably the most captivating co-op game ever released, offering an engaging single-player experience alongside an excellent multiplayer offering. And now you can play with friends on a host of different platforms.

WORLD OF TANKS BLITZ

Supporting players across Android, iOS, Mac, and Windows 10, *World of Tanks Blitz* pushes its players into huge tanks and gets them to battle it out in historical battlegrounds in groups of seven.

POKÉMON GO

Get yourself out and about with *Pokémon GO*, the game that pushes you to pursue pocket monsters all around your local environment. One of the best parts of the game is the ability to battle and trade with anybody around you, regardless of whether they are on the same platform as you or not.

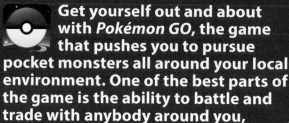

HEARTHSTONE

Hearthstone is truly the most accessible and entertaining competitive card game ever created and, thanks to its awesome online support, you can enjoy it on the move with all of your friends, regardless of what device they are playing on. It's a high-quality game that only gets better the more time that you invest into it.

FROST

A GAME WITH SPIRIT

Frost delivers puzzle-solving on a galactic scale, yet keeps things about as simplistic as possible. Each level begins with hundreds of tiny spirits flowing into view and you must use your finger to draw a path of salvation to their home planet. Quickly, twists come into play: multiple species and planets, unbreakable barriers, and other dreamlike diversions. *Frost*'s difficulty gradually increases, but these challenges won't leave you feeling cold—this inventive game creates a warm, relaxing sensation, perfect for unwinding.

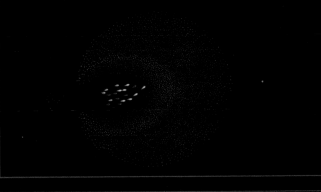

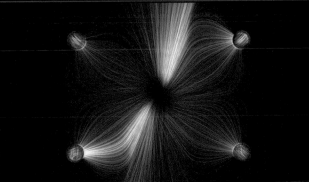

FAST FACT

Developer Kunabi Brother describes the various sights in the game as "Neutrino Flowers," "Glowing Baitballs," "Supergravity Shepherds," and other intricate creations.

The space spirits are represented as little flowing dots. While simplistic in design, the resulting look is pretty stunning in motion.

TIPS & TRICKS

EXPERIMENT OFTEN
Frost's challenges require trial and error, so don't feel bad about a botched attempt: that's how you learn.

BUILD BARRIERS
As stages become more complex you may need to separate different parts of the screen. Consider building walls using provided streams of light.

DON'T MUTE IT
The compelling sound effects help elevate the experience and add more life to the minimal graphics.

LIKE THIS? ALSO CHECK OUT…

BLEK
Blek, the *Frost* creator's earlier puzzler, is a mobile classic. You'll work to solve puzzles by drawing tiny scribbles, which then mimic your input and crawl across the screen. There's nothing quite like it.

PRUNE
Prune is another methodical and mesmerizing game, one that tasks you with summoning a tree from the soil and guiding it toward sunlight by carefully snipping unneeded branches as it grows.

VIKINGS: AN ARCHER'S JOURNEY

ARROW-SLINGING ENDLESS RUNNER

When endless runners were invented, they had one control option: tap to jump. *Vikings: An Archer's Journey* shows how far the genre has come. As well as leaping, it lets you pull back on the screen and unleash a torrent of arrows at your various enemies. Collect brightly colored runes along the way for points. Success means rewards—there are five different Viking characters and lots of brilliant power-ups.

For the tips box

TIPS & TRICKS

COLLECT THE RUNES
You're more likely to succeed if you pick up runes. They can let you enjoy exploding arrows or even slow down time.

DON'T SHOOT EVERYTHING
If you are building up a combo and you misfire with a shot, the combo attempt will reset.

PULL RIGHT BACK
Want your shots to be powerful? Think about putting some elbow into it. Drag your finger back as far as you can before unleashing.

FAST FACT
Vikings: An Archer's Journey was made in France by Pinpin Team and it has been downloaded more than two million times. The same developers also produced *Pyro Jump* and *Anark.io*.

As well as watching out for glowing collectibles, you need to keep your eyes on the ground and the sky for foes heading your way.

LIKE THIS? ALSO CHECK OUT...

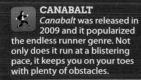

CANABALT
Canabalt was released in 2009 and it popularized the endless runner genre. Not only does it run at a blistering pace, it keeps you on your toes with plenty of obstacles.

AB CLASSIC
The original *Angry Birds* was a breakthrough hit thanks to its unique gameplay. It used a slingshot to launch birds at a castle—aim perfectly and you destroy it.

GLOSSARY

GO GAMING! ▼

GEOCACHING
When your mobile uses location data to show your position in the real world and reveal items and characters based on that position.

IN-APP PURCHASE
An item you can buy within a game, using real-world

IRL
In Real Life.

JRPG
A role-playing game developed in Japan, and often translated into English.

MANA
Characters that can use magic within a game will

FREEMIUM
Freemium titles are free to download, but offer in-app purchases that will allow you to play more easily.

ACCELEROMETER
A tiny chip in your phone or tablet that can recognize small movements of the device. This can be used to control a game, such as steering a car in a racing title.

ANDROID
Google's mobile operating system, which is used on millions of phones around the world.

APP STORE
A virtual store through which you can buy and download apps and games for your devices. For iPhones, this is simply called the App Store. On Android, this is known as the Google Play Store.

AUGMENTED REALITY (AR)
Apps that use your device's camera to show an image of the world in front of you, and then overlay game elements (like creatures or items) onto the world.

CODING
The act of writing code. Code is what makes up every computer program and game—learn to code and you can make your own games.

ESPORTS
A type of game where players can go head-to-head against each other in multiplayer competitions.

money. These can include in-game currency, new characters, and levels, or extra items for characters.

IOS
The operating system used on Apple's iPhone and iPad. This system is only available on Apple's own devices.

consume mana as they perform spells. Collecting more mana will recharge their magical powers.

MANAGEMENT SIMULATOR
A game genre in which you oversee and manage many different things at once.

ENDLESS RUNNER
A game genre that doesn't have a final point to reach. Your character runs in a never-ending world and the goal is to go the farthest distance or set the highest score.

PAY-TO-WIN

A criticism sometimes leveled at multiplayer games. If a game features in-app purchases that offer powerful weapons, better characters, or extra skills, people who pay to purchase these items have a better chance of winning.

PROCEDURALLY GENERATED

Levels that are created by the game as you play, based on a series of rules and calculations. They will often appear to be quite random, and no two levels will ever be the same.

MECH

A large robotic suit that can usually be entered by a human and controlled, giving the character more shielding and more damaging attacks.

METROIDVANIA

A genre of action-adventure game with gameplay concepts similar to the *Metroid* and *Castlevania* series. These games feature large, interconnected worlds, and require players to gain upgrades and new abilities to unlock new areas.

MOTION CONTROLS

A control system that utilizes the accelerometer and other motion sensors that are built into your smartphone or tablet. You can tilt, swing, or shake your device and the game will convert this movement into actions on-screen.

MOD

A modification that changes the way a game is played.

MULTI-TOUCH

Most modern touchscreen devices allow for multi-touch technology. This means you can place two or more fingers on a screen and complete an action to see results in the game.

RHYTHM GAMES

Games which have you tapping in time to music to score points. The better your timing, the higher your score.

ROGUELIKE

A genre of games that typically feature 2-D pixel graphics, a high degree of difficulty, and procedurally generated dungeons. These games are inspired by the 1980s game *Rogue*.

SANDBOX GAME

An area in which the player is given the ability to choose what they do and when they do it. These games often include building and creation aspects, and usually take place in large, open-world environments.

SMARTPHONE

A mobile with a touch-based interface, internet access, and an app store. A smartphone combines these features with normal mobile abilities, like the option to make phone calls.

STEAMPUNK

A fantasy world in which advanced steam-powered technology is common. Usually, games in this genre mix old-fashioned styles with powerful computers.

TABLET

Tablets are often like larger versions of smartphones, but without the same phone capabilities. They have larger screens, and often more powerful processors inside, which can produce better graphics.

TOUCHSCREEN

The main interface used on smartphones and tablets. Most modern touchscreens react to even the softest touches.

VIRTUAL REALITY (VR)

A technology that allows you to place your smartphone in a special headset and hold it up to your eyes. Your phone creates an image for each eye, so it feels like you are looking around the world for real.

TOWER DEFENSE

A game genre that sees on-rushing enemies trying to attack and destroy your base. You must place defensive towers strategically to stop the attacking hordes before they reach you.

VIRTUAL D-PAD

A term used to describe the on-screen controls that mobile games often use to help you move characters around the screen.

XP

Experience Points. Gaining enough of these in a game usually results in a character moving to the next skill level and getting better abilities.